SUPERGEDDON

What People are Saying about the Right Behind™ Series

"The most profitable Christian fiction series ever, except the 66 canonical books of Scripture. Printed by Gutenberg and still printed today. Have them in stock or face obsolescence, irrelevance, locusts, and boils."

—Publishers' Biweekly Smart Business Tip #665

"Sock and Wilson are doing for Christian literature what Wal-Mart did for convenience stores. . . . The greatest epic series since Homer . . . his lack of foresight allowed only one sequel."

—TEMPORA ET MORES

"The authoring committee's style keeps the reader stuck on every page, as on flypaper, with a kind of horrified fascination."

—Christian Temple Marketers Asso.

"Combines bargain thrills with light pastels of romance, high-tech naivete with the holy aura of a televangelist's wife's coiffure. In short, complex."

—The Unspecified Times

"Definitely not preachy. At all. Not one bit. Almost as opaque as the book of Revelation itself."

—TV Blind Guide

"It's not your ancestors' Christian fiction anymore. Buff Williamson has more whoopass in his can than Ehud, David, Beowulf, Arthur, Sir Guyon, Henry V, Raphael, and Captain Ahab put together. Okay, *Moby Dick* isn't Christian fiction, but still. . . ."
   —The Dallas Seminary Endofthedays News

"So popular that we have to mention it and yet tread softly so as not to alienate our readership."
   —USA Tomorrow

"The bit about the Antichrist getting stuck between the toilet and the tub [in *Right Behind*] was crass and tacky. Not funny at all."
   —Heather Wilson, wife of author

A * REALLY * BIG * GEDDON *

SUPERGEDDON

DR. SOCK

NATHAN D. WILSON

UPTURNED TABLE PARODY SERIES
CANON PRESS • MOSCOW, IDAHO

Nathan D. Wilson, *Supergeddon: A Really Big Geddon*
© 2003 by Nathan D. Wilson

Published by Canon Press
P.O. Box 8729, Moscow, ID 83843
800–488–2034 / www.canonpress.org

07 06 05 04 03   9 8 7 6 5 4 3 2 1

Cover mimicry by Paige Atwood
Cover Image: Carousel Gone Testy

ISBN: 1–59128–013–3

Library of Congress Cataloging-in-Publication Data

Wilson, Nathan.
  Supergeddon : a really big geddon / Nathan Wilson.
    p. cm.
  ISBN 1-59128-013-3 (pbk.)
  1. End of the world—Fiction. 2. Armageddon—Fiction. I.
Title.
  PS3623.I5856S87 2003
  813'.6—dc21

                              2003013157

To Chris LaMoreaux
Whose lips first shaped the immortal word
Supergeddon

Special Thanks
to Queen Elizabeth
for her expertise when the techie bits got sticky

MANY WEEKS INTO THE TRIBULATION;
FEWER WEEKS INTO THE MORE SERIOUS
GREAT TRIBULATION THAT'S QUITE A BIT
MORE INTENSE THAN JUST THE NORMAL,
RUN-OF-THE-MILL TRIBULATION, THOUGH
BRIEFER:

*The Good Guys, weighing in at 2,834.24 lbs. and
more than 1500 hit points*

Buford Tin, mid forties; former flight attendant, three-time winner of the Pan-Continental "Spirit Award"; became available after losing his wife in the Rapture. Also lost twelve-year-old Little Bufie, his will to live, and a timeshare; former chief steward for the biggest bus on the Duke de Lafayette's "Farewell America" tour; founding member of the Tribulation Farce acting troupe; international fugitive; able to disguise himself convincingly as a Gypsy. Best power move to watch: Scissor Kick.

Cameroon "Buff" Williamson, early thirties; Ivy League graduate; youngest ever senior writer of any major weekly in the history of the world; slightly pudgy; played the female lead in all three of the Tribulation Farce's first productions; webmaster of andrewsullivan.com and editor of *In the Buff*, the most popular webzine ever, ever; bruises easily and occasionally introduces himself as Jeff. Favorite book: *Billy and Blaze.*

Cleo Tin-Williamson, early twenties; former student, Mayville Community College; lost mother and brother in the Rapture; wife of Buff; daughter of Buford; owner of chinchilla Kenny Bruce; CEO of International Creative Memories Cooperative, an illegal underground network of Baptist pastors; author of *Out of Africa* and *Birds of Nova Scotia*; looks good in baby blue. Favorite thing: brown paper puppies tied up with springs.

Simon Ben-Tribeofjudah, world's greatest philosopher/theologian ever; makes the apostle Paul and Augustine look silly; dealing with an internet addiction; more hits per day on his site than people still living; current spiritual leader and e-pope of the world; would like to meet nice twenty-something Caucasian for movies and something more than friendship. Favorite pick up line: "We don't have long to live."

Dr. Heinz Rosenbeet, smartest Jew ever; occasionally goes by the name Mikhail; unlocked the genetic secret behind mass zucchini production; Nobel winner; murderer of the world's chosen leader, but it was pre-conversion so it's all right; attracted to fuller-figured women. No power moves.

Leah Rosa, greatest ER nurse in the state of Illinois since the state's induction into the Union; would like to meet and fall in love with the world's greatest philosopher/theologian ever. Hobby: anonymous web chat.

Place additional throwaway Arabic character here.

Max Maxmillan, late fifties; presumed dead in a fluke bowling accident; unknown purpose in the story; friend of the author.

Hannah Shinymoon, late twenties; yet another nurse; inspiration to young Native American persons everywhere; provides author emotional sense of literary diversification in later books; wonderfully shapely; got her start in soap operas; dated the author's son in college. Biggest inspiration: Chesty Puller.

Ming Chong, early twenties; generically-named female Asian; world's leading authority on Belgian Female Incarceratory Technique. Hobby: collecting shells.

Chang Wonton, seventeen and a half; generically-named male Asian; world's greatest DOS programmer; first ever Asian to beat the Russians at travel-size Connect Four. Once hacked into a bank's reader board and changed the temperature and time. Power move: Hot Dragon Soup with Luck Punch.

Flavius Josephus (a.k.a. "Zeke" or "Tiny-Z"), early twenties; greatest forger ever to come out of Nigeria; got his start in Bond films; currently living in Iowa coaching junior high wrestling. Graduate of DeVry with an A.A. in disguises.

Alexandre Dumas, dead; author of *The Three Muske-teers.*

Georgio Seabass, old; pathetic dying Cuban fisher-man; Roman Catholic; lost in the Rapture the biggest fish ever hooked.

The Really Bad Guys, Weighing in at 129 lbs. and 3,000 hit points

Randy Jarvis, late thirties; former Tulsa native. WLTM nice woman fond of scarlet. Interested in world domination. Has a habit of raising himself from the dead and cohabits his body with Satan. Favorite band: Pedro the Lion.

And various other bad guys.

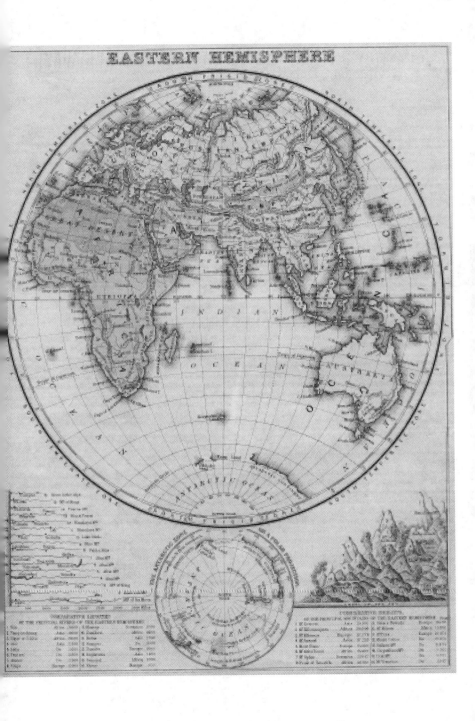

EASTERN HEMISPHERE

PROLOGUE

From The Tenement

"I AM THE EVILEST people ever!" Randy Jarvis said. "Or is it 'most evil'? Director Akkbar, which is it?"

"Evilest."

"Great. Thanks. In this, the excerpt from the previous book, I am making plain my utter villainy. I am encouraging you, my sort-of hangers-on, who have been with me through the trials and travails that come with eleven puffy-paged books, to bounce back. The oceans are no longer blood; they have scabbed completely over. There are no such things as fish; the AC guy tried to claim that mobile homes are just harder to cool, but I talked him into a new unit anyway; I thought up a great new joke about Jews; and our plans for the extermination of all decent folk are finally shaping up."

Randy's new mood lasted only three days. Then the lights went out. Literally, and I'm not joking here. No, really, if you flipped the switch in the kitchen of your trailer, the five bulb chandelier would just sit there looking at you blankly, completely unresponsive. If you walked into the living/TV room, you would have no more luck with the dimmer switch by the door. Give me a minute and I can think up a whole list of light-emitting things that no longer emitted anything light-like: cell phones, Christians, nightlights, flash-lights, headlights, key lights, garage-door code pads, expensive calculators, headlamps, Maglites, laser pointers, blinking children's toys, Ferris wheels, stars, and the aurora borealis. The entire New Babylon Villas Park was in darkness. And not just the normal sort of darkness that happens nightly all over the world, but the kind of darkness that happened to you in fourth grade when you crawled into your sleeping bag head first, got stuck trying to turn around in the end, and nearly suffocated. We're talking about an oppressive darkness. You may think that I might be just about wrapping up the description of this dark-ness, but I'm not. I mean this was some dark black kind of darkness, like go into the basement, squeeze beneath the stairs, kill the lights, and pull a paper bag over your head kind of darkness. If you were to have some reason to put your hand in front of your face, you probably wouldn't have been able to see it.

Nose-picking in the mobile villas of New Babylon became very difficult. Well, maybe not, because most people remembered where their noses were.

But I'm not done. Road flares, phosphorus, radon, lightning—none of them shone. It matters not what I'm going to say next; it probably won't give off light either. Birthday candles? Ha! Everywhere people in New Babylon groped their way to chemical cabinets in search of elemental magnesium, and when they found it, they continued their groping to the toilet and dropped the elemental magnesium into the bowl in dime-sized pieces, and then they waited for that telltale pink fireball that always comes at such times. But there was no pink fireball. There was only a small plop, some brief hissing, and a noise like a squeaking armpit.

Everyone in New Babylon got a rash from handling so much magnesium.

Chang Wonton is a generically-named Asian male. He lives in New Babylon Villas, and he was the exception to this whole darkness business. When he opened his fridge, he didn't even have to strain to see the pickles. True, the light in the fridge didn't work, but he could still see. And he didn't have a rash because he was never even tempted to handle magnesium, let alone throw it in the toilet.

It was to no avail. [Note to editor: is this appropriate here? Could you look up *avail* for me? I like the line a lot and it means a great deal to me, so if it doesn't seem to fit here, please stick it somewhere where it does.]

Chang laughed out loud a lot in the darkness. Mostly because he could see, and the other people couldn't. He found that funny. He knew that practically everyone in New Babylon was a loyal Randy Jarvis groupie and deserved all the darkness he/she got. They even deserved the rashes. Chang also laughed because for some reason the author decided that he had to see in sepia tone. The darkness didn't affect him like it affected everyone else; it just turned the world a golden nostalgic brown—something that had to have been prophesied somewhere. It struck him as a little odd that everyone in the trailer park was wearing period costumes from the Old West and the Civil War, but he took it in stride. Things were always a little strange in New Babylon.

After a couple of days of walking the streets of the park and laughing when other people tripped on speed bumps, Chang got the most brilliant idea that anyone has ever had, ever. And Chang is a smart guy. He's Asian, for one thing, and he is the number one computer smart guy in the entire world. Though he might not be smarter than the hot Jewess he'll meet a little later on. [Ed.: That's just a little technique I've developed to keep the reader interested. I call it "foreshadowing."] So anyway, Chang had an idea. And it was terrific. Better even than the time he bred his own subspecies of gypsy moth in Chinese junior high. What Chang thought was this:

"If all these people can't see, then I can take all their stuff. Everything!" For the first time since Book

Eight, it looked as if the good guys might get a break—
a break full of stereos, satellite receivers, Playstations,
and laptops.

Right when he thought his thought, Chang realized
how important the darkness was, and how great it
was to be able to see in sepia tone. He dropped to his
knees with the necessary religious fervor and begged
God to give him more time.

"Time is all I need! Time and a hand truck! Then
we'll rake it in on e-Bay."

ONE

BUFORD TIN PLAYS MARCO POLO WITH THE ANTICHRIST

FOR THE THIRD time since takeoff Buford Tin offered his friend and pilot, Abdul Smith, a Seven-Up.

"You nervous, Bufe? You never offer me Seven-Up unless you're nervous."

"Yeah, I'm nervous," Buford said. He never would have said that before he was a believer, back when he had only believed in things he could touch, smell, weigh, and eat. "We shouldn't have brought her, Smitty." And he glanced furtively at the controls.

"Don't touch them, Buford."

"I wasn't going to."

"Someday I'll let you touch them, but not yet."

"Ha!" snorted Buford. "When? Before or after Supergeddon?"

"Before."

"I'll hold you to that, Smitty. I get to touch the

controls before Supergeddon."

"Deal. Now what do we do with her?"

"Her? Her who?"

"Her. You said we shouldn't have brought her."

"Oh, you mean Naomi? But she's pretty."

"I know that, but you're the one who said we shouldn't have brought her."

"So?"

The AOL Cessna 7.0 blazed its way through the Middle Eastern skies on a direct course toward a mobile home park outside of Baghdad. Chang had called in air support. He was smart enough to know that he wasn't going to get away with that many TVs on a camel. The plane was more than big enough for the five-hundred-plus televisions, DVD players, Playstations, and X-boxes, along with the one really nice standup freezer Chang had managed to swipe. But there were only two seats, the pilot's and copilot's, and Abdul wouldn't allow anyone to sit up front. Naomi and Buford played cards on the floor behind the pilot's chair. They could have played tag in a transport plane that size, but they didn't. They did occasionally offer Abdul some nuts. They called him Smitty, because that's what people sometimes call other people whose last names are Smith. I only know one person whose first name is Smith. Sometimes Buford or Naomi would just yell out "Hey Smitty!" just like that, and then they would both laugh. It was lots of fun. Smitty didn't mind; they were close like that.

When Abdul first spotted the darkness over the trailer park the plane's clock was just chiming 1200 hours, Standard World Order Time. The normally glimmering trailers were completely hidden, and there wasn't so much as a hint of an astroturf lawn.

"Bufe, Naomi, come take a look at this."

"What?" Buford said.

"There is an amazing darkness hovering exactly on the park."

"Isn't that what Chang said?" Naomi asked.

"But shouldn't it just look kind of brown to us? I mean if we can see in sepia tone?" Abdul's concern was obvious.

"Let's not worry about the details. I'm sure the copyeditors will smooth them out later." Buford had read more books than the other two, so he understood that sometimes this sort of thing simply happens.

"I have a question. But I'm not sure it's appropriate. It might be a little out of character," Naomi said. Well, her real name is Cordelia but she plays Naomi. She's not even Jewish; she's Italian. Close enough.

"Go 'head," Abdul (not an actual Arab; real name: Julio Gomez) said. "They can dub it later."

"Shoot," said Buford.

"Do you guys really believe this stuff? I mean that a big pile of darkness will come sit on a trailer park outside of Baghdad?" Neither man answered. "C'mon, what do you really think?"

"Cordy, we could lose our contracts. We're not supposed to talk about this stuff," Buford said.

"You said they would dub it."

"They could dub it. If they didn't fire us first."

"I think this kind of thing could happen," Julio said. "I mean God does amazing things all the time."

"I don't think the issue is whether or not He does amazing things. The question is whether or not He does corny things."

"Guys," Buford said. "This conversation is making me uncomfortable."

"Because you are afraid for your job?" Cordelia asked.

"No . . . it's just that—well, I don't like to think about these kinds of things."

"Why?" Julio asked.

"Oh, c'mon Julio, you know why. I'm all embarrassed now."

"No, I don't know why. Why?"

"I'm an evangelical. I mean, so are you guys, but—"

"You are?!" Cordy's surprise was apparent from her punctuation.

"Aren't you?" Buford sounded oh-so-hopeful.

"No."

"You, Julio?"

"No, but my mom was a Catholic."

"Well then, what are you guys? Why are you here?"

"Secular gigs are hard to come by. Bufe, is your name really Buford?"

"Yeah."

"And when, you know, we're talking and stuff, you know, in the story, you aren't really having to act, are you?"

"No. Are you guys really just here because you can't get into secular novels?"

"Well, this is good exposure," Cordelia said. "I'm sorry, Buford. I hope we didn't ruin it for you."

"Okay, campers, back in character." It was Abdul and he was on the pilot's PA system. "Shake it off, Buford."

Normally, the noonday sun was pretty bright, but as the plane began to descend and prepare for an initial approach, the brightness diminished. It shrunk, it dwindled, it gradually ceased being the big bright noonday sun and became a dull brown. Sepia brown, but badly developed sepia.

"Do we need an ILS?" Buford asked Abdul. "Don't you think it would be a good idea? We can't afford to let down Chang. After all, he's been our mole inside New Babylon for quite some time, and has been very effective. He has been really good with recording all conversations for the last two years and burning them onto secret minidisks and then transferring them, using his own brilliant adaptation of OLE software, via websites that rotate every certain number of seconds, to my own laptop back in San Diego. It has been really helpful listening. I've learned so much about working through difficulties in marriage, especially from that one couple, the Brahmins."

"It would sure be a shame to let him down now.

Naomi, why don't you call him on his specially encrypted phone? It is on a random satellite rotation so no one can trace it. Have him meet us in the goat pasture south of the park. I have to figure out what ILS stands for and land this plane."

"Do you have an infrared port on the dash there?" Naomi asked.

"Of course," Abdul said. "What do you take me for?"

"Then point my palm pilot at it, and it will ask you where you want to land. I'll call Chang." Abdul took the palm pilot and pointed it at the infrared port.

"AOL Cessna 7.0, ahoy," the palm pilot said.

"Wow," Buford and Abdul said together.

"Where would you like to land?"

"Ibn Sam's goat pasture."

"Excellent choice. I can text message a warning to move the goats. Would you like to play Tetris? I play Tetris very well."

While the plane continued to descend and Buford played Tetris, Naomi was on the phone with Chang. She was realizing something. Chang had a very nice voice. While this might not surprise us, it did her. She had only ever instant-messaged him with her computer questions. You see, she was the head of the tech center responsible for all of Tetra, where many of the world's true believers were hiding from the chaos raging across the glue blobe and wielded by the mighty hands of Randy Jarvis. She ran bulletin boards and chat rooms, and posted the joke of the day on the front page of their site. So she always had questions. But now she heard the voice of the man who always had answers. Just this instant it was saying, "It's amazing here, Naomi. I won one hundred and fifty Rands today just betting people I could guess how many fingers they were holding up in the dark. I don't know that I want to leave. And I never win at basketball. Today I took another twenty Rands betting on pickup games. I still couldn't make a basket. But they couldn't tell, I just kept yelling "Swish." I can't wait 'til you get here—I can't get anyone to bet on singles ping pong. They're playing doubles only. You won't believe the rashes on some of these people."

The plane came shrieking out of the sky real dramatic-like and touched down in an almost text-book goat-pasture landing. Thanks to the text mes-sage the goats had all been safely moved. But rashy people were a little more surprised. We can't really know how they ended up in the pasture, but they were practically blind, so I guess wandering into a pasture isn't that farfetched. When they heard the shrieking engines, they did a little shrieking themselves and ducked and ran for cover, itching and scratching all the way. When the plane came to a stop and the door opened, Buford, Abdul and Naomi found Chang and his stack of stuff waiting for them. He was a natural looter.

Buford looked around at all the blind people lining the fences.

"They're chewing on their tongues? Why would

they do that? That's gross."

"They're preparing for the Great Battle, the Supergeddon. Our website says it's less than a year off."

"What does that have to do with it?"

"They have to chew their tongues first. I'm not sure why."

"Hey, c'mon guys! We've got some time, and I want to show you around. It really is great." They all followed the excited Chang out of the pasture, stopping only once, to watch Chang trip an overweight man trying to figure out where he was.

"This trailer park is like nothing I've ever seen. We've got a pool and foosball, there's a place where you can check out croquet sets, and there's Bingo on Wednesdays. Is it Wednesday? I could do some real damage at Bingo in this darkness."

"I think we should split up," Buford said. "I somehow have the impression that it's the orthodox thing to do upon arrival in a strange place. We should separate and meet back at the plane in two hours."

"Great," Naomi said. "I'll go with Chang."

———

Buford was glad when the others had gone. He hadn't had any real time to himself since that morning, and he was a guy that needed time to himself. That's what he had always said whenever people asked him. When he was at parties and people would say, "Hey Buford!

Do you ever need time to yourself?" he always responded in the affirmative. But even though finding someplace quiet and taking off his socks to let his toes dry out sounded good, all the betting money to be made in this town of darkness was also attractive. In the end he took his shoes and socks off, and then went out in search of members of the local blind populace who might be interested in a flutter.

The first guy he met agreed to race him down the street for five Rand. Buford won easily and the money changed hands. He beat three others at thumb wrestling, though two of them refused to pay, and he found a woman willing to bet that he couldn't tell what color her eyes were. He lost that one when he guessed "sepia," but he was not discouraged since the afternoon remained a net gain.

It was then that he found himself at the sporting complex and aquatic center. He was disappointed that no one was playing racquetball, or anything else for that matter, but there was one guy in the pool. Buford almost spoke to him but stopped himself in time. The man in the pool was glowing. Not too much—just about a three-foot radius of glow. He was glowing and muttering to himself something about air conditioning and mobile homes. Buford didn't even need to consult the script to discover who it was. He knew already. This was the supposed Antichrist. The man who had found a way to whisk off all believers and cotton in Book One. The man who had kept them hidden all this time. The man who had hypnotized the

United Nations, who had sold more carpet than anyone in the history of his hometown of Tulsa, and who was now running the entire world from a small trailer park outside of Baghdad.

"This," Buford thought to himself, "is a moment not to pass up." With that he slowly removed his clothing until he stood at the edge of the pool wearing nothing but his tighty-whities and a big grin. But how to get in without him hearing? Buford located the nearest stepladder and swiftly and silently ran on tip toe toward it, his belly quaking with excitement. When he arrived he caught his breath. The Antichrist still had no hint of his presence. For all he knew he was alone in the pool with his thoughts. First one toe and then a bunch of others. Buford's legs were in up to his calves and still he was silent. Then it happened. What always happened to Buford when he got too excited. He had held his breath too long and his body suddenly acted on its own in its need for oxygen. He snorted loudly and without warning, and fell the rest of the way into the pool.

"What! Who is that?" the Antichrist yelled, but Buford didn't hear him because he was under water and had banged a fleshy knee on the bottom rung of the stepladder.

Buford surfaced into immediate panic. The Antichrist had already moved toward the sound. He was only four feet away and approaching. Buford lunged to the side and dove under water. Once under, he tried to double around the Antichrist. He did, and slowly eased his head above the surface. He had shaken him. The Antichrist was facing the other way. And then it came. The Antichrist had called out, unmistakably. . . .

"Marco!" the Antichrist sang.

"Drat!" thought Buford. He was a Christian and knew he had to follow the rules, and so, in a voice swift and punctuated he cried out, "Polo!"

Just after one o' clock in the morning in San Diego, Buff Williamson fell out of his hammock. As he picked himself up off the floor, Cleo stirred. "Stop messing around, Buff. You have no respect for others." He did not answer but froze on his hands and knees. "Buff, get back in bed." He held up a hand to silence her. "Buff, I said get back in bed. You need your sleep."

"Shhhh."

"Buff. I want you to get back in bed right now. You need your sleep."

"Shut up, Cleo."

"Buff!"

"I said shut up."

"Buff, you know better than to talk to me like that. What would little Kenny think if he heard his daddy talking like that?"

"If you don't shut up, you'll feel the back of my hand."

"Buff!"

"Cleo, I mean it. I thought I heard something."

Providentially, at this point Buff's walkie-talkie
chirped from the nightstand and prevented what could
have turned into a nasty domestic disturbance.

"That's the secret code that means Big Jorge sees
something through the periscope in the southeast
corner of the perimeter," Cleo said.

"You think I don't know that? I came up with the
code! Stay here." Buff leapt to his feet and headed for
the door. "Say 'Roger,'" he said. "I said 'Stay here.'
You have to say 'Roger.'"

"Roger," Cleo said, and Buff was gone.

Five minutes later he was in Jorge's camper shell
looking through the periscope. Since Randy Jarvis had
announced that anyone who revealed the location of
any true believers would receive a lifetime twenty
percent discount at the global online food co-op, Buff
and Cleo Williamson, along with their eight-year-old
son Kenny and thirty-two others, had all been hiding
out in a deserted camper shell dealership ten miles east
of San Diego. They had dug holes and tunnels all
across the lot, covering them with camper shells and
tarps. It was very inconspicuous. Jorge, a former
Coast Guard member, had even successfully purchased
a periscope online and had only mounted it on his
shell the day before. That way he could look around
the lot without leaving the comfort of his hole. But
you always had to be careful. The Navy had gotten rid
of the periscope for a reason. It always squeaked when
you turned it—it was simply a question of whether or
not it sounded like a merely angry squirrel, or a

squirrel losing its toes in a bird feeder accident.

"I don't see anything important, Jorge. There are some Hummers unloading Babylonian Loyalist troops, but I doubt they're looking for us. I've always wanted a white holster like that. Did you see their holsters?"

"No," Jorge said.

"Take a look." After his look, Jorge agreed that they were nice holsters. "Well, I'll be going back to bed. Lemme know if there's any real trouble."

"Sure," Jorge said.

When Buff crawled back through the dirt tunnel and into the camper that he and Cleo shared, he tried to get back into their hammock without waking her up. He couldn't.

"What was it?" she asked.

"Just some BLs, probably looking for a drive-thru open late."

"Yeah, or some pornography," Cleo said.

"They had really nice white holsters though. They must be a new issue." And with that, Buff was asleep. Cleo, however, was only waking up.

"White holsters, eh?" she thought to herself, and eased out from beneath the blankets. "Maybe I ought to take a look." As she dropped to her knees and squeezed her large frame into the tunnel, two hammocks swung behind her. Little did she know that, unless this author changes his mind, she would never see those hammocks swing again, or the lip gloss she left on the nightstand, or even the San Diego Zoo. For her, the game was just about up. She had gained too much weight and simply wasn't an appealing character anymore. No one really knows why she had let herself go to seed like that, but she had, and authors must take steps in such circumstances.

When she got to Jorge's camper, he was asleep on the dirt in the corner. Luckily he had left the periscope up. She took a quick peek. Nobody. Just a bunch of Hummers. "Huh?" she thought. "I wonder where they could all have gone? Maybe I should check, just to be sure. She crawled to the tunnel exit and lifted the tarp. No one. She crawled further. Still no one. She sat back on her haunches and twitched her nose a bit. Nope. All clear. She wondered if the soldiers had left any snacks in the vehicles. How happy everyone would be if she had some snacks for them in the morning, and they didn't know where they came from! She wouldn't tell them. They thought she was fat, but she knew that she was really quite sneaky.

The Hummers were unlocked. The first three were completely empty, at least of food. There were lots of documents, but nothing tasty. The soldiers from the fourth Hummer were apparently pretty odd; there was a large aquarium in the back of theirs. In the fifth Hummer, she struck pay dirt. The entire rear of the truck was full of supplies. Good-to-eat supplies.

Half an hour later, two Babylonian Loyalists opened the rear door of their Hummer.

"Well, if it isn't Cleo Williamson," said one, who was a little more in charge than the other. Cleo was unconscious, her face covered in peanut butter. "The boss said peanut butter would do the trick. He saw something in her dossier about it. All we had to do was lace it and leave it. No need to cuff her—she won't be waking up until 11:41 tomorrow morning."

"Marco!" The Antichrist called out. He was already zoning in on Buford and was slowly bouncing up and down and side to side in the water with his arms out as far as they could reach. It was a nice pool, but small, and Buford was getting worried.

"Polo," he almost whispered. And then the Antichrist lunged as fast as a short thick man can when he's up to his chest in water. Buford was bigger, but his feet weren't gripping the bottom! He was slipping in place! Nowhere to go! He dove to one side, Randy was right with him, there was no way he could make the corner. He faked back the other direction but slipped and went horizontal, barely saving his toes by grabbing the edge of the pool and pulling himself tight against the concrete lip covered with small tile. The Antichrist came on, grinning. Buford was almost in his glow now. The Antichrist would see him!

It must be admitted that at this point, Buford stretched one rule and broke another. He pushed off the bottom as hard as he could and leapt as far out of the pool as he could. Skivvies sagging behind him, he clawed with a strength that can only come with the adrenaline of a near loss at a pool game, and he left three fingernails behind.

"Fish out of water!" Randy yelled. That was the rule Buford stretched, depending on what part of the world you are from. Now, as clear as could be, at least before the darkness started, there was a big sign posted in the aquatic center. It was screwed to the wall right above the place where the long net hung for fishing things out the pool, and right beneath the clock. In red letters at the top, it read "Swim at your own risk." Beneath that was a "No diving" and beneath that a "No running." And Buford was undoubtedly running. He was, of course, using the classic light-on-the-conscience twinkletoes run—lots of leg revolutions and no striding. The Antichrist was also running at this point but nobody could expect *him* to follow rules. Buford, however, was a Christian. And of course, as always happens when people sin, calamity struck. Buford heard the laughter of the pursuing fiend shift into a sudden squeal. He turned and saw the fall of the Antichrist. There is always a reason for rules. Always. The Antichrist had slipped; his feet came out from under him and continued their ascent until they were above him. It looked briefly as if Randy might land it on his bum, but that brief moment passed in over-rotation and all possibility of a happy ending for the sad incident faded. Randy took it squarely on the shoulder blades, at least until his head snapped back and hit the floor.

"Crap! Oh sorry, strike that," Buford said as he carefully hustled back to the white and quivering body. "Um," he said. "Randy? Are you okay? Randy?"

That's when Buford saw the blood. "Crap! Crap! Crap!" he said. "I hate mortal head wounds."

TWO

IS THIS KIND OF LIKE A DICKENS NOVEL?
Or
KIND OF LIKE A DICKENS NOVEL, ONLY BETTER
Or
BETTER THAN A DICKENS NOVEL
Or
HOW TO BUILD A DECK IN A WEEKEND

CHANG AND ABDUL were sitting on the steps of the plane watching the goats graze. Naomi was on Chang's lap.

"Just scoot over a little. Your bottom-bone is digging into my thigh."

"Where do you think Buford is? It was his idea to split up." Abdul is the one that said that.

"Don't worry, Abdul. This is always what happens. It wouldn't flow if someone wasn't late."

"Yeah, but we're also supposed to be worried."

"Not all of us."

"I hope he's okay," Naomi said. "He's like a father figure to me."

"How long have you known him?" Chang asked.

"That doesn't matter; you get to know people so quickly in these last days."

"Is your real dad dead?" Abdul asked.

"No, but he's so oppressive. He's back at Tetra with Heinz Rosenbeet, Simon Ben-Tribeofjudah, and all the other supposedly saved Jews, munching what they are calling manna and drinking spring water."

"I've never been to Tetra," Abdul said.

"I saw U2 there last summer. It's a huge amphi-theatre," Chang said. "I'm looking forward to seeing it again."

"Yeah? Well, I'm sick of it. I wish Supergeddon would just come already, and we could start getting this whole millennial kingdom thing over with."

"It sure doesn't look like it's going to be long coming," said Abdul. "Simon Ben-T has more than a third of the world's population logging on to his website every day, and more than a whole bunch of Jews with him in Tetra. I saw online that the Anti-christ has been posting want ads all over the world for horsemen to lead his charge through the valley of Supergeddon toward Tetra. Applicants have to be willing to travel within ten days, so that gives us a pretty solid time frame."

"Simon told his cyber-congregation yesterday that Christ will come back about fourteen minutes into the battle. You know, his website has the highest traffic of any website in the history of the whole world. There are over one billion daily hits, and there hasn't been a single server problem despite the collapse of the entire globe and the deaths of over two-thirds of the earth's population," Chang said.

"Where is the server? Couldn't Randy just blow it up or something?" Naomi asked.

"Servers are things? You mean tangible entities with spatial and temporal extension and location? I thought they were spiritual. Why haven't the bad guys crashed it?" Abdul asked.

"Because," Chang said, "they can't find it. It is currently hidden inside my cell phone. When I was working more closely with the Antichrist in his royal trailer complex, I had it a little better hidden. I had it inside a hearing aid epoxied into my navel, which is surprisingly deep for a guy my size. When I moved it, I had to crack the hearing aid in half because I couldn't get the glue to give. Half the hearing aid is still in there."

"Is that Buford?" Abdul asked. "What's he bringing? A goat? We don't need goats."

Buford had broken quite a sweat lugging the Antichrist practically across the entire park and a little way out of town. Then he had happened on a large she-goat. After a quick drink he had draped Randy's still wet body across the goat's back. Things were a little quicker after that upgrade. As he led the goat up to the plane he could see the confusion on his friends' faces, and he wasn't really sure how he would explain this.

"Who's on the goat?" Chang asked.

"What's on his head?" Abdul asked.

"Is he all wet? Why did you take all his clothes off?" Naomi asked.

Buford decided to take the approach of the con-
queror. "This," he said, "is the Antichrist. I found him
in the pool."

"He drowned?" asked Chang.

"Um, no. He was running poolside and slipped and
cracked his head."

"Is that wet underwear on his head?" Abdul asked.

"Yeah, I was trying to stop the bleeding. It's all I
had handy. You see I was in the pool too, and, well,
yeah, he slipped."

"I can't believe the Antichrist wears a red Speedo."
Naomi was obviously shocked. "It looks like he
shaves his legs, but his back is pretty pelty."

"You better put him back before he comes to. Or
just leave him on the goat. We shouldn't be here once
he's conscious." Chang was nervous.

"Well, that's not going to happen. He's pretty much
dead." The other three just stared at Buford. "My
underwear wasn't that effective stopping the bleeding.
When his pulse stopped, I tried CPR, I really did, but
it didn't do a thing, and when I pumped on his chest
more blood just came out his head."

"Why is everybody acting so glum? Doesn't this
mean that we win already, and without the big fight?
Why would you even try to save him, Buford?" Chang
was still just a baby Christian.

"We're screwed." Abdul had been a Christian
longer.

"I really did try," Buford said. The goat bleated.
Naomi pulled the underwear off Randy's head.

"Oh my," she said. Chang passed out.

———

When dawn came to San Diego, she found a group of some thirty-odd believers huddled in a hole under a camper shell, weeping.

———

"Will he fit in the freezer?" Chang asked.

"Easily. We don't even have to fold him. Where's the palm pilot? I need to get this thing off the ground." Abdul's initial depression at the Antichrist's death had begun to fade, and he was now his professional self. "Buford, I'm gonna need a beverage service in about twenty." Buford wasn't listening. He was looking at the face of death, propped up in a standup freezer.

"How do we keep him from falling over and knocking the door open? Wouldn't it be easier if we just laid this thing on its back?"

———

They took turns weeping all morning.

———

"No," Chang said. "Because, as I have already told you twice, Buford, this is a standup freezer. If we put it on its back, it will leak freon. I want this thing working when I sell it." The engines roared to life.

"I'm going to need you folks to take your seats and fasten your seatbelts, if you don't mind. We're heading for Tetra," Abdul said.

"Won't Simon Ben-T mind if we're bringing the Antichrist into Tetra?" Naomi asked.

Cleo sat up suddenly. She was in a cell, wearing an orange jumpsuit. The walls and ceiling were painted purple. "Randy Jarvis Rules!" had been painted across the ceiling in large white block letters. It was also on the back of her suit, but she couldn't see that. The bars of her cell were also white, and there was no window. The floor was gray, but seemed to have some really small pattern painted all over it. She got down on her knees and looked closely. The floor was covered with endless lines of "Randy Jarvis Rules!" in cursive script. There was a toilet in the corner, and it apparently served as a sink as well. Apparently she had been sleeping on a shelf-sort-of-thing against the wall opposite the bars.

"Not much to do in here," she thought to herself. "At least I can see the TV out in the lobby." And she scooted over to the bars to get a better look. "This isn't going to be that bad." But she hadn't met Flo. Flo is the large bipolar black woman of indeterminate job description. She has a cell phone and is occasionally

44

seen with a mop. This time, as she approached Cleo's cell, she had a wad of keys.

"Boss wants to see you," she said, and unlocked the door. "Get yourself on up now." Cleo did, and the two of them lumbered down a long corridor, stopping in front of a door with the number 333 scrawled across it in red. Flo knocked and opened the door. It was completely dark in the room. It was almost as if someone had turned off the lights, because, as it turned out, someone had.

"Sit down," a voice said. Cleo fumbled her way into the room and found a chair. The door slammed behind her.

"Do you have an aquarium in here? It smells sort of like fish." A flashlight flicked on and lit up a large aquarium teeming with crawfish. The light flicked off again. "I . . . I—that's the aquarium I saw in the back of the Hummer. Then you're . . . you're . . . ."

"Yes," the voice said. "I am. I had you brought in because I need some information."

"What?"

"Well, of course I'm interested in all your compatriots and their locations. And their phone encryption systems. But more than that, I would really like to understand the evangelical psyche. Why the heck do people read this stuff? I mean, there's never really a plot; the narrative structure resembles a mini-series; the characters redefine superficial. Is it just bad writing, or is that how evangelicals are? And they really believe this sort of thing is going to happen?"

"I'm not talking!"

"Have you breakfasted? Would you like a sausage? I have some right here."

"That would be very nice." The sausage changed hands. "You know I've never really understood the evangelical thing myself," Cleo continued. "I mean I really am one, but I'm not sure I understand it all. It seems really important to us that we lose every fight and then kind of get bailed out in the end. I mean, the world goes to pot, and then all the Christians disappear, it keeps going to pot, we keep losing and then we get bailed out again right before the big battle."

"Isn't it *during* the big battle?"

"Maybe. Anyway, can I have another sausage? Thanks. Do we need to leave the lights off?"

"It's better this way. Where do you keep the server that supports Simon Ben-T's inflammatory web site?"

"Last I heard, it was in Chang Wonton's navel."

"His navel?"

"Glued in. With epoxy."

"But Chang is one of ours. He's a top guy in New Babylon, he works directly with the Antichrist! Does he know it's in his navel?"

"Oh, yeah. He's been one of us this whole time. You mean you haven't been reading the books?"

"Chang Wonton! I can't believe it."

"Of course you can. You've read the script." Cleo's head began to swim. If the room hadn't been black she would have been able to tell that the room was spinning. "Something in the sausage," she said, and fell to the floor.

Jacques pressed a button on his phone (his name was Jacques). "Flo, can you come drag her back to her cell?"

It took Flo a while, but she got the job done.

———————————

When the sun was high over Tetra, things tended to get a little warm and sticky, and the million or so Jews that had congregated at and around the amphitheater had a tendency to get a little testy. Most of them had met Simon Ben-T (the world's greatest theologian, endtimes expert, mayor of the Tetra remnant, and *People* magazine's Sexiest Man of All Time), as I call him, in various chat rooms. The man was forever online, assuming different personas and convincing innocent and lonely people to "join me in the beautiful and exotic desert around Tetra. Drive due south into Edom and take a left at the first road after you see the flying snakes." New people showed up every day.

The sun was high now, and three men huddled over some quail eggs they were frying in the sand. They could tell that Simon was coming. Everyone could always tell that Simon was coming. Everywhere he went he took a bullhorn. He said he kept it with him so he was always ready to proclaim the truth. The bullhorn actually had the effect of familiarizing most of Tetra with Simon's mouthbreathing. And his singing voice.

"Manna time! Hey! Hey! Manna time! Manna-mannamannamanna time!" Simon did not take kindly toward people eating anything outside of collective meals, so the three men quickly tossed back the underdone eggs and headed off toward the feeding place.

Tetra was no Thomas Kinkade village. There was very little happiness here, though there was lots of light. There were also lots of rocks, a bunch of hastily erected equipment sheds full of four-wheelers purchased on the Middle Eastern black market, the amphitheater, modular homes, and tent sections. Somehow Simon had arranged for thousands of modular homes to be flown to Tetra from Chicago. Some of them had even been furnished. The tents were mostly from REI lootings. But despite the thousands of tents and homes, many people still preferred to sleep by campfires, which they built for s'moring purposes every night regardless of the heat. Simon didn't like s'mores, so it was all done on the sly. Which wasn't too tough due to the bullhorn.

The people were slowly funneled into the amphi-theater, grumbling as they took their seats. It was a miracle it happened three times a day. The mob that Simon numbered at 1.234006 million sat down to eat in an amphitheater capable of seating only twenty thousand, and all of section C remained empty. Then the prayer began via bullhorn, and midway through the prayer the large gun that Simon pretended was not behind the stage would go off. It was an air mortar and three times a day it strewed Nilla wafers atop the assembled. The Nilla wafers and the water from the fountain above the theater were all that Simon provided his friends, but he insisted that God miraculously tampered with the wafers to make them completely sustaining.

The air gun was firing the food for the third time when Buford and Abdul's plane screeched above the theater, leaving contrails hanging mere feet above the ground. They were landing just outside of the camp but would taxi into one of the temporary hangars. Simon went to meet them. He knew who was in the plane—at least all but one—and what the mission had been. He was looking forward to a new laptop and installing satellite TV in his modular compound.

Naomi was the first off the plane. As always, Simon admired her figure.

"Hey, Simon. Dad's not around is he?"

"No, I don't know where he is."

"Good." Naomi reached back into the plane and pulled Chang out by the hand. "C'mon, I'll take you up into the cliffs and show you the best make-out spots. There's a great one we call "The Ravine" though technically no one is allowed there after dark."

"Why's that?" Chang asked.

"Too many babies," Naomi responded. And they left, holding hands and skipping lightly with the joy of their faith, humming worship tunes as they went. Naomi's faint "I choose to be holy, / I choose to be set apart for God" was still audible long after the two had disappeared into the rocks.

"Ah, kids!" Simon said. "Oh, to be young again! They don't seem to even realize that the world is falling apart around their shoulders and clinging to their shirts. I hope they realize that now is a really bad time to get married."

"Hey, Simon." Buford was standing in the door of the plane.

"I preach on it all the time. 'Don't get married,' I say. But they can't listen. Only fourteen days left of existence, and they want to get married. Hey, Buford, welcome back. How'd it go?"

"We've hitched our wagon to a star."

"What?"

"Or our star to a hitch."

"I'm not sure I get your drift."

"I know the word hitch is in there somewhere, and I think it's functioning as a noun. We've struck a hitch? But you don't really strike hitches. Anyway, Simon, we have a problem."

———

Cleo came to more gradually this time, for which she was appropriately grateful. Why she should be grateful, I do not know. Nor how appropriateness would play into it. Regardless, she regained consciousness. The first things she did were some hamstring and groin stretches, because she was feeling a little tight. Then she scooched her way to the bars and tried to

watch TV. The TV wasn't on, so she just sat there and
waited patiently, hoping someone would turn it on.
No one did. Flo came by once and laughed at her.
When she had left, music kicked on, apparently piped
through invisible speakers. The sound quality was
excellent, as was the performance. Flo had turned on
the radio in the middle of this piece, sung by the New
World Chorale and composed by Randy Jarvis himself
under direct inspiration from Satan.

Randy, Randy, he's so handy,
Extra cute and also dandy,
Insert phrase about mint candy

Chorus
(write chorus later)

Randy, Randy, he's so hot
Something, Something
Fill in later,
Smile like an alligator

[Ed.: Is this a poem? I've heard about poems
before, but are they the same things as songs? I think
this one is pretty good, but it might need to be tight-
ened up a bit.]

After the song was a recruitment ad for horsemen
with experience in end-of-the-age battles. After that,
there was a little news flash.

"Cleo Tin-Williamson has been apprehended in her

mansion in San Diego. Authorities say that Cleo was operating one of the most difficult and economically impossible operations in the history of the world, a global marketplace in which no one pays for anything. This of course is illegal. She also has refused to take on the mark of the beast. 'With the marks currently available to choose from there is absolutely no excuse for this kind of behavior,' authorities said. Most women prefer the small butterfly on the hip underlined with the name "Randy." Second is the sun in the small of the back. Roses and dolphins are available for ankle placement, and Mandarin Chinese is available for shoulders. When asked why she would not take the sign of Randy Jarvis, she replied that she was already marked for heaven, produced a Strawberry Shortcake sticker from her sock, and applied it to her head in the name of God. 'See,' she is reported to have said, 'This sticker is my baptism, this is my sacrament, my death and resurrection.' Despite Cleo's apparent role in the assassination of the Antichrist in Book Six or Seven—one of those middle books—she might not stand trial due to insanity. Instead she would be used for shampoo testing and eventually freed."

Cleo leapt to her feet. "Slander!" she screamed. "Libel!" she hollered. "I never said any of those nasty things, I never even heard of half those words. They're just trying to make me look stupid! I'm not insane! I just got lonely and found my sticker! I can take it back off!"

Flo stepped out from the shadows. Wait a second. What could cast a shadow large enough to encompass

Flo? Anyway, Flo stepped out from the shadows that were somehow, well, on the walls.

"I'm sorry, baby," she said. "I just bought myself a chocolate shake. Would you like it?" Cleo didn't answer, she just nodded and wept. The shake was passed through the bars. Five minutes later found her once again wandering the strange corridors of a drugged sleep. But somewhere in there was a mind, a mind enfeebled but trying to write poems about love, childhood, and firsts of summer camp.

———————

Jerusalem hasn't come up once in this book. Has it? There really is no excuse for that. Here we are, plowing through a book about endtimes, and big-doings all round, and Jerusalem gets the cold shoulder. Well, no more.

Al was one of the top three black marketers in the entire Middle East. He was ranked third in the Associated Press poll, second in the coaches' poll, and second in *USA Today*. He was a well known and classy, sneaky guy. There wasn't much he couldn't do or get. He had once successfully acquired top-secret technology from Langley, Virginia that enabled the wiring and remote control of a cat. This he had not sold but had held onto, waiting for a time when he might desperately need it for himself. That time had never come, so the necessary equipment was in a closet somewhere. Al had also done a roaring trade in semi-vital organs and stolen pets. He was known by all who know black marketers, and to know him was to respect and love him.

He lived in the Old City, because otherwise why are we talking about him? The Wailing Wall and other historical sites were very near and dear to his heart. He had always lived faithfully toward God but simply had never heard of Jesus Christ. Was that his fault? Was it his fault that you never gave to support missionaries, and never stuck your money in the appropriate bucket on missions Sunday? If Al were to die before converting, which—who knows?—he might do, just whom exactly to you think deserves to burn? Al? You? Does your money mean that much to you? Checks can be made out to: Innocent Heathen Defense Fund, mailing address: 205 E. 5th, Moscow, ID 83843 (USA).

So Al lived in the Old City. His parents apparently weren't fond of his infant face, and so they left him on the steps of what they thought was a Catholic mission. It wasn't. It was a bar, but the two can be difficult to differentiate. Young Al got his start in the black market when one day a man stopped him in the street and said, "Where can I buy a baptism? Or any sacrament really. Please someone! Please!" Of course, this being the story that it is, Al was unable to help him. But that's unimportant. Anyway, he is one of the top three black marketers in the region, and one of them died last week in a fluke rollerblading accident, and the other guy is really mean. So I guess Al is actually one of the top two guys.

But enough about Jerusalem.

"Chang, are you thirsty?"

"A little bit."

"Why?"

"What do you mean why? We're in a desert."

"I'm sorry, I got the wrong line." Naomi was sitting up on a rock. Chang was sitting on the same rock, facing her, but there was a slight incline—not too bad, but noticeable, so that his head was decently lower than her own. This facilitated the fingers-through-his-hair thing that was currently going on.

"There's a spring right near here. Would you like to drink from my hands?"

"Mmmm," said Chang. So they went to the spring.

"What the—uh, heck are we supposed to do? Blinkin' prophecy is blamin' out the window." Simon spoke with passion. He was a natural actor and was even able to make the language restrictions of this book sound natural and convincing. "Buford, you're pathetic. Do you realize what you have done?"

"I didn't really do anything."

"You have let down God! He is weeping—mourning this horrible calamity! You have completely thwarted all plans that He had for the end. There is now not even the least need for Christ to return and free us from disaster, because there won't be a disaster. We won't be getting slaughtered and so we won't need to be rescued. I wouldn't be surprised if this has totally undermined God's plans for the opening week festival of the millennial kingdom. Most of it was scheduled to be praise songs, in nearly eternal loops, describing His overthrow of the Antichrist. But now, how impressive is that? Big deal, God. Overthrowing the Antichrist was quite an accomplishment. Buford already did it by cheating in a swimming pool game!"

"I wasn't cheating."

"You mean you were in the only pool on this earth where running *is* allowed?"

"The sign said swim at your own risk."

"Did it say run at your own risk?"

"Simon, I think we should decide what to do." It was Bruce talking. He was from Wisconsin and had first met Simon three years ago in a lactose-intolerant chat room. Simon had been calling himself Gabby then. Now Bruce was the chief R.A. of the entire tent sector. "I'm sure Buford is sorry."

They were all sitting in a large tent. There were thirteen of them breathing. On a table in the center lay the frail dust that once housed the soul of Randy Jarvis. He was still wearing swimwear, though some-body had managed to strap the back of his head back on. Naomi's dad spoke up.

"Are we positive it's the Antichrist? He doesn't

have the mark of the beast."

"He doesn't have the mark of the beast because he is the beast. He doesn't need to demonstrate self-loyalty. And, yes, I am sure this is the one. I have wrestled with him in many visions, including a pretty weird one last night," Simon said.

"What was it?" Bruce asked.

"Well, first off, I was back in junior high and was walking around the school in my little red wrestling suit and ear protectors. Somehow I ended up at the match, and then there was Randy all suited up as well and ready to wrestle."

"So what happened? Who won?"

"Well, you know, it's hard to say, because my ankle's been bothering me a bit and I wasn't quite at my usual quickness."

"So he won?"

"Well, not really."

"Why not really?"

"I mean he did pin me three straight times—but my shoes were really slippy—so the ref called him the winner, but he ended up getting an infection from some bacteria in the mat. I mean who do you call the winner after that?"

Naomi held out her cupped hands to Chang.

"Were you going to fill them with water?" Chang asked.

"Oh yeah." Then she extended them again, and he drank. It was hard without getting water all up his nose, but he did it. "How was it?" she asked.

"It was okay."

"Can I drink from yours?"

"Sure." Chang filled his hands and she drank. When she was done he ran his wet hands through her raven hair. It took a while, because personal hygiene wasn't one of her strengths. When his hands returned safely, he dragged them down her forehead to her cheeks. His thumbs found her eyelids and closed them slowly. Then he rested the weight of his thumbs on her eyes and rolled them around, feeling the shape of her eyeballs. He applied more pressure.

"Ow! What are you doing, you nit?"

"The eyes are the window to the soul," Chang said.

"Can you stop?"

"Sure." And he did. "Naomi? Can I ask you a personal question?"

"Yes."

"Do you think premarital sex is always wrong—I mean in every situation, even at the end of the world?"

"Yes."

"Oh, I do too," he said quickly. "I was just curious."

THREE

PINCH HITTING FOR THE ANTICHRIST

Buff Williamson answered his cell phone on the third ring. He was pushing little Kenny in a shopping cart. Not in a store—just down the sidewalk.

"Buff Williamson, world-record-holding journalist, editor of the second most important web site in the world . . . how can I help you?"

"Buff, this is Simon. We've got a little problem over here. In fact I'm a little concerned that your father-in-law—you knew Buford was Cleo's dad, right?"

"Yeah, I found that out. Go on."

"Well, anyway, Buford may have actually botched all of reality. This whole story of life might now have a bad ending."

"What could be worse than a gradual deterioration of goodness culminating in a collective good guy cop-out, followed by newly recruited good guys getting

59

their butts kicked all around the globe, followed by yet another copout, and the distribution of the participant ribbons?"

"I'm not talking about literature, Buff. I'm talking about history here."

"So am I."

"Do you have a little grouch this morning? What's wrong with you?"

"Cleo's been captured and will probably be executed."

"Yeah, I heard about that, but it's no big deal. You'll see her again within two weeks anyway. I don't think this world has much more than that left in it."

"Oh, I know Cleo is no big deal, but we lost our compound because she may have compromised us."

"So what are you doing now?"

"We're all pushing all of our earthly possessions down the sidewalk in stolen shopping carts."

"Buff, you're a great guy, but—and this is said as a friend—you've always been a little caught up in earthly possessions. Why don't you just let them all go? You can't serve God and mammon, you know. You have to make your choice."

"Right. Sure. What did you need, Simon?"

"I need you to fly to New Babylon and impersonate the Antichrist."

"Why?"

"Because Buford killed him." Buff heard a faint voice in the background over Simon's phone.

"He says it was an accident," Simon relayed. "But

in the meantime, we have an endtimes battle to prepare for, and we are not going to be able to do it without an enemy. We need you to go and continue Randy's work for him. We need evil to culminate, and the logistics of getting the whole massive battle thing together, with the two hundred thousand horsemen and all, has got to be a nightmare. There's no way it's going to happen without an Antichrist at the helm of the world."

"I don't want to be the Antichrist."

"You wouldn't be. You would just be pretending to be him, doing what he would have done anyway. It would only be make-believe, you wouldn't really have to be evil."

"Fine."

"Can you be here by two o'clock? We'll brief you then."

"We don't have a plane, Simon."

"Pretend. You have a blessed morning."

Tiny-Z was the greatest makeup/costume artist in the world. This in itself was quite an accomplishment, but even more impressive is the fact that he was self-taught. Now it may seem odd to be introducing a new character at this juncture in the book, but I assure you that it is not that odd. At this point I need a makeup/costume artist, and so I introduce one. As it turns out, I have needed one in previous books as well, so Tiny-Z isn't exactly a new introduction. I also will be needing a top black market man at some point, and I anticipated that nicely by introducing the reader to Al in the last chapter. You see, with really great authors, no word is out of place or without purpose. Yak. Anything that is done is done intentionally. It is all part of the pattern that will eventually be made clear once you can view the sweater in its entirety. Once, and quite recently, I had the pleasure of viewing an actual sweater worn by an actual man. At first I must admit that I was concerned for the man wearing it. But as I stepped back, tipped my head a bit to the right and squinted, it all became clear. It really did sort of look like a Polynesian fertility god. At least if someone had told me that it was one, I wouldn't have been able to dispute. So I may say 'yak' now, and you may find yourself confused, but just shake your head and chuckle. Tell yourself, 'That's the trouble with great authors. I might think it's just a yak, but later on I'll find out that it was actually a fertility god.'

Tiny-Z had been a truck driver, but he wanted to rise to new heights, and soar like a seagull. And, I'm told, seagulls can't fly with only one wing. So Tiny decided to take a correspondence course from DeVry on disguises. He did, and graduated at the top of his class, successfully disguising some apocalyptic fiction that Buff had written as actual storytelling for his final project. He connected with true believers at a Green-wich soiree and ended up costuming all of the Tribula-tion Farce's off-Broadway productions. From there it was a mere step to his participation in all of the other many neat adventures that you can read about at your leisure in my other books. I'm sure you'll agree with me that Tiny-Z's work has been quite impressive.

Simon had called Tiny immediately after talking to Buff. He had been at a mascot convention, getting some great exposure. He hadn't wanted to fly to Tetra to dress Buff up, but Simon was persuasive, and Tiny finally agreed.

———

Buff brought the entire San Diego cell to Tetra. He was the first one off of the plane and pulled his shopping cart and son behind him. The lighting was perfect and he was framed very nicely by the plane and some distant rock formations. He waved to Simon amid the flashing of cameras trying to capture the perfect publicity shot. Simon and several others were there to meet him. Behind Buff came Jorge and Haddie the Whore of Babylon.

"Haddie!" Simon yelled. "What's she doing here?" Buff seemed confused.

"What do you mean? I told you everyone was coming."

"She's not in the story any more, Buff!"

"Why not?"

"Well, didn't she die or something, way back, in one of the middle books?"

"Of course I didn't," Haddie said. "Would I be

here if I had?"

"Haddie!" Simon said, "I will not jeopardize my position on this cast by admitting that you're alive or here at all. I apologize, but professionally I cannot afford to speak to you, though you do look lovely, and once the story has switched elsewhere once more, I would like it very much indeed if you would join me in my tent for drinks. Now Buff, we need to settle this." Simon looked around at all present. "Does anyone here have a copy of the books?" There was no answer until an intern spoke up.

"She never died, she just had the Antichrist's baby. She's not a believer. She never made the transaction."

"Well, thanks for that much, I guess," Haddie said. "I know I haven't died, but to tell the truth I don't remember much else about my role in the story. I was working in a lot of other stories at the same time, and doing lots of talk shows, so it's all a bit of a blur."

"Right. Well," said Simon, "We might need to order the CD-ROM Illumina Edition online. Then we can have the complete text of all the books available for word search, as well as some spectacular charts and timelines, all of which can be seamlessly integrated with another important book, the Bible. That should settle the question quickly, but in the meantime, we can't be too careful, and I'll need you to stay out of sight, Haddie. Now I've got a big sermon to download off of homiletics.com, so I will see you all later. Buff, we'll be briefing after chapel."

"Chang, this backrub feels great, but I really should get back to work. We have to prepare a pirate feed onto every TV station in the world for Simon's lesson today, and I still haven't posted the joke of the day."

"I can post the joke while you hack all the appropriate satellites. Would that help?"

"That would be great, Chang. I like the way your name rolls off my tongue. Chang."

"Chang doesn't really roll."

"Sure it does, listen . . . Chang."

"It sounds like you dropped a cookie sheet."

"But a round one that rolled around a bit."

"Well, I'm glad you like it. You know it's funny that I like you so much. I always thought that I would be different than all my friends, and that when it came time I would break that age-old Asian stereotype, but here I am fulfilling it once again, just another Asian guy falling for a Jewess."

"Ha! Well, think of me! It's even worse for me. I always pushed for liberation. My father was so oppressive and demanding. No matter what he told me to do, I pushed the other direction. That's part of the reason why I'm so attractive. But here I am, doing exactly as I was told."

"What do you mean?"

"Well, he always used to sit me down and explain to me, 'Mimi,' he used to say—that's what he called me—'Mimi, you are a Jewess and I will expect you to behave that way. I don't want you thinking you can get out of your duty; you will marry an Asian just like all the other respectable Jewesses.'"

"That's rough."

"Yeah, the only thing I hate about you is the gratification he will get from mebeing with you."

"If it helps, I'm not circumcised."

"Not for long, if Simon hears about it."

"Ha! How would he hear about it?"

"I'll tell him. C'mon, I can hear the bullhorn."

Simon was always overcome with emotion before a performance. It didn't matter that he was the greatest theologian since the Apostle Paul. Well, that's what people said about him. But he knew that he was able to see things in the text that Paul would never have dreamed of. Or any of the Apostles really. John the Revelator seemed to have a little more difficulty explaining things than Simon knew he would have. But he had to work with those who had gone before him, though he always enjoyed himself the most when he was preaching completely on his own, without a text, and simply reaching into the very lungs of reality and forcing it to cough things up. Today, his message would be powerful, and he knew the question-and-answer time afterward would be impassioned.

When he stepped out in front of his million or so,

he knew that they were not the only ones watching him. Billions around the world were tuned in whether they liked it or not. They must listen, and through his voice they would find repentance. He knew that in these times even the angels were listening. They had read Revelation as well as he, and no doubt found the book as poorly expressed as he had. If even they wanted to know what was going to come to pass, then they would have to join his congregation. Simon knew that he personally must have been prophesied some-where, and he leaned toward Psalm 24, though he hadn't made any public announcements yet.

He raised the bullhorn to his lips, and then, with all the power and the might that was in him, he spoke, and his speech was like that of angels, his wisdom was that of Solomon's, and his voice rang with an author-ity only matched in the voice of a female traffic cop.

"Next time the devil!" he shouted. "I said next time the devil comes knockin' on your door, ask him where he got that knot that's on his head. Say, 'Oh devil, where did you get that knot? It's seems to be all black and blue and pussing! It must hurt so much, Brer Devil, where did you get it?' He won't answer at first, he'll try to pretend that he just slipped on some stairs, but we know better. He got it in the Carmen song!"

[Ed.: I'm finding this whole sermon composition thing a bit exhausting. Are there any interns handy who could just stick in a bunch a verse numbers, and copy some things from a couple study bibles? I think about eight pages would be good. Verses about Christianity would be especially relevant.]

When Simon finished, he was able to make his voice sound almost hoarse, and all of Tetra was in tears. There had been altar call after altar call, and the conversion counselors had been kept very busy. They had all been personally instructed by Simon, and so they were very good at reassuring people that "This is just like a business transaction. Agreeing to sell your lawnmower is no different. We have you sign this card here, and say these words out loud, but you can still renege if necessary." Or, "Come on, just say the words, it will be fun."

"Let's open it up for questions. Are there any questions?" Simon asked the mob. "Yes, you in the front. Yes, use the bullhorn on the stand there." Then the little man in the red cardigan spoke.

"Yes, Simon, thanks. First I just want to thank you. I'm a big fan and have all your albums. I was wondering, you know, if God can marry Israel, and then sort of not really divorce her but separate and marry the Church, then marry Israel again too . . . well, I'm wondering why I have to get kicked out tomorrow for polygamy. Why is that? I mean my wife behaved almost exactly like Israel, but she's back now, and I still have my second wife. What's the big deal?"

"Ted—your name is Ted, isn't it? Right, okay, Joseph. Well Joseph, you're a real ass. If there's anyone who annoys me more than a person who will take another person's premises and things and try and draw conclusions from them, then I haven't met them yet. God and Israel and that whole thing—that isn't real. Christ doesn't really marry the Church. It's just a metaphor, a picture."

"Of what? I thought our marriages were the pictures, and they were supposed to be picturing God's."

"Just shut up, stupid! Dumb-bottom! Nobody but a dumb-bottom would wear that sweater. Anyone else? And please, stick to serious questions. I've had a long day. Yes, Fontina."

"Thank you so much for your ministry, Simon, I think you are a most courageous man and I wish you would consider remarrying."

"Well, I am considering it, and I do think that Scripture is clear that men in positions of leadership can have multiple wives, and concubines even, while little men in red cardigans can't. And I know there are hundreds of women here, and more online that I chat with every day who would love to fill those roles. And, when it comes down to it, my tent is large, and I have an additional modular compound, but thus far I haven't taken wives simply out of pity for them. I do not want to break a thousand hearts when we would undoubtedly not be in the same social strata in Heaven. Yes, you all the way in the back, go ahead."

"Yeah, just how much blood will there be at the battle of Supergeddon?"

"That is a very important question. There will be a standing body of blood that will be four feet deep and one hundred and eighty-four miles long. I am still praying that the exact width will be revealed to me."

When Cleo came to, she found that she had drooled so much in her sleep that she was terribly parched. And there, sitting on the floor next to her, was bottled water. "Hmm," she thought to herself. "I wonder why the seal on the cap has been broken." And she drank. Soon thereafter her head hit the floor heavily. Jacques and Flo stepped out from behind something or other and stood looking through the bars at Cleo. Jacques's look was concerned.

"Flo."

"Yeah, boss?"

"She's one tough cookie. I don't know that we'll break her. I've never seen a prisoner so . . . so . . . unflappable. So highly trained."

"I know, boss. I've spent a lot of time thinking about her personal fortitude. I even wrote a little sketch about it. It's all about how I want daughters like her, and . . . and . . . ." Flo wept. Jacques put his arm around her shoulders.

"I know, Flo. I know. I've been thinking the same thing about my sons." His shoulders began to shake. They wept in each other's arms. They wept until their faces were slicked thick with grief, and then sleep, that comforter of the sorrowful, came to them and brought peace. It left behind two heavy, mouth-breathing piles on the industrial tile beyond Cleo's bars. Making three total.

The Jerusalem sun warmed Al's ears. He hoped he would hear from Simon soon.

Cleo shivered on the floor and almost came to. Flo and Jacques stirred not.

In a mere four hours, Tiny-Z had successfully transformed Buff into the epitome of all evil. He coached him in mannerisms and eyebrow motion until his perfectionistic standards were met. He even matched some of the Antichrist's most famous suits from his mobile wardrobe. He knew that no one could see in New Babylon, but he wasn't taking any chances. And besides, even if no one else knew that Buff didn't look like Randy, he would know, and his conscientious [?] would bother him. His professional conscientious was very tender. Buff, a perfect Antichrist, was bustled onto a helicopter and flown off to that thick patch of darkness that had already played host to so many adventures.

Darkness fell swiftly on Tetra. It wasn't anything
special. It was just night. But it was dark. Stars were
sneaking in and out of a couple of desert clouds.
Simon had finally drifted off in his compound, the
bullhorn slept, and s'moring had begun around a few
thousand campfires. But there was one tent, the tent
where the leaders met, that had no campfire in front
of it. Nor was anyone inside it. At least not anyone
other than Randy Jarvis. He had been laid on the table
in the middle of the tent for examination by the
leaders. When they had all been convinced that he was
actually the Antichrist, and Buford had been repri-
manded, he had been shoved into a large plastic bag
and left on the table. The burial crew would come by
in the morning.

That plastic bag, full of evil, on the table in the
middle of the tent, now stirred. Was it a breeze? Was it
some evil thing come with the darkness? Something
was afoot. The bag now did more than stir. It jerked
and lurched, it quaked and snapped, but there was no
wind in the tent. Then the bag fell off the table onto
the fake sheepskin rug and stopped. But not for long.
It wasn't jerking now, it was expanding, stretching,
growing thinner. A tear opened at the top and out
came four fingers, followed by a hand. Then another
hand. Both were followed by arms. A head emerged,
slowly and painfully, wrapped in cloth. Before long
the entire body crawled its way out, a body wearing

nothing but its own flesh and a red Speedo.

"Mother?" it said. "Mother, are you there?" And then, exhausted, it collapsed into a deep sleep.

"Chang, are we necessary to the story at all?"

"We're relatable characters. We make the books more marketable."

"But how do we affect the plot? Do we?"

"Is there a plot? Things happen, sometimes we do things—you know, hacker things, or young people things, and so we're necessary. We fill a demographic need. I wouldn't be surprised if characters like ours were required in the author's contract."

"Chang, will you stay with me after the story's over? I don't like to think that you are playing a part and that's all."

"Just watch the s'mores."

"Cleo, I'm afraid we're going to have to kill you. We're going to take you to Joliet and guillotine you. The blade is rusty and nasty, and a large crowd will cheer. We'll even broadcast it on international television so your friends can watch, but an angel will come and blind the cameras, so no one will see when it actually happens." Flo leaned over to Jacques and whispered in his ear, "That's what happens in the real book."

"What happens in this book?" he asked, turning to Flo.

"We don't know yet. We just got orders from New Babylon that you are to be made president of the Christian Writers Guild, but we're not sure how to do that. I mean, do we just write them a check, or what? So we're waiting to hear more. We'll let you know."

"But I can't write."

"I don't think it matters, honey. It's not really about writing."

Buff sat at his new desk. It was a simple enough affair. Veneer something or other in the back room of a brand new double-wide. The air conditioning seemed a little funky—one minute he was shivering in a freon breeze and the next he felt like a pork loin wrapped in foil being slow-grilled by indirect heat. [Note to editor: Once the final product placement contracts are signed, insert a brand name grill above. I would prefer it if Weber worked out, but I don't have any scruples about going elsewhere.] The Antichrist had no messages on his answering machine and only two emails. There were, however, a stack of horsemen applications three feet high in his inbox. He had begun his work there and had started calling through references when he had an idea. He was the Antichrist. He could free Cleo. But he wasn't sure if he was supposed to. "I'll call Simon and ask him if I'm allowed to do that sort of thing."

"Hello, this is the prophet of the millennium."

"Simon, I have a question. Should I free Cleo? I mean, here I am, king of the world, why should I let my wife be executed?"

"What Would Antichrist Do?"

"Well, he would kill her, why does that matter?"

"Buff, you're there impersonating the Antichrist, not to get information or pull strings, but to fulfill prophecy and keep this whole thing on schedule. You cannot abuse your position. It wouldn't be fair to Randy."

"Who cares if we're fair to Randy?"

"I care, Buff. I have a conscience. He wasn't supposed to die, but Buford monkeyed around. Randy paid the price, and he stood to lose a lot. Do you think it is fair to him, now that we've already cheated once, to keep on cheating?"

"I see what you mean."

"You were one of the best journalists in the world—okay, the best journalist in the world. You know what it's like to be neutral and objective. You can't take either side, you have to ask yourself, 'What would Randy do?' and follow your conscience."

"You think I should have my own wife executed?"

"What would Randy do?"

"He would subject her to a fate worse than death."

"What do you mean?"

"I mean torture. What if I appointed her as president of the Christian Writers Guild?"

"Good God! You would do that to your own wife, the mother of your son?"

"You told me to be objective and neutral. I am no longer Buff. I am an instrument of prophecy."

"Follow your heart, Buff."

———————

Simon hung up the phone and inserted it into the folds of his tunic.

"I'm reeeeady!" He sang. "I'mmmmm rea-heh-heh-dy, ready to put onnn my lonnng white robe. Reeeeady! Hey Bruce, Buff seems to be doing well. Bruce, look over there." And he pointed. "Is that who I think it is? How could I have been such a dunce! What Scriptures did I miss?" Bruce followed the quivering finger to the flap of the leadership tent. There, blinking in the sunlight, stood a small man, his white skin burning brightly in the desert sun, his eyes shielded by a hand.

"Mother!" he cried. "Where are you?" Simon put his hand down as the figure (it was in fact Randy Jarvis) began wandering off between the tents, calling for his mother. His walk was jerky and his feet burned on the sand. He stopped and stared at one of the camp's four-wheeler ATVs parked outside a tent.

"Are you my mother?" he asked.

"Randy," Simon said. He and Bruce had walked up behind him. He put a hand gently on his shoulder. "Randy. It's okay, we haven't left you, we're right here. Come on, Randy, let's take you inside and let you rest in the shade. Would you like a drink?"

"Are you my mother?" Randy asked, and his eyes filled with tears.

The leaders were gathered all throughout the tent, sitting and standing and kneeling. Some were even lying on their sides with their heads propped up on their hands. Others were on their bellies. Simon sat cross-legged in the center, with his arm around Randy beside him. Randy was finally clothed. Someone had done a better job bandaging his head, and Bruce was questioning him slowly for all the leaders to hear.

"What is your name?"

"Randy."

"How old are you?"

"Six."

"Where do you live?"

"I live in the blue house."

"What town?"

"Tulsa."

"Are you the Antichrist?"

"I play first base. My mom gave me a bat for Christmas." Bruce looked up at all the leaders.

"It's almost worse than if he had died. We can only pray for a complete recovery and restoration of his memory."

"So, you were Jeffrey's landlady?" Buff asked.

"Yes, he's a good boy. Loves horses."

"Does he have his own?"

"Yes. Well, it's more of a pony."

"Ah, and how do you think Jeffrey would look in thigh-high black boots?"

"Um, I don't think the boots have been made that would fit over Jeffrey's thighs."

"He's large, then?"

"Yes."

"How is he with a sword?"

"I don't know that he has ever touched one."

"Okay, thank you very much, Mrs. Lunders."

"Oh, you're welcome, Mr. Jarvis." Buff hung up the phone. He really wished he hadn't had that talk with Simon about objectivity. He was trying so hard not to cheat in his hiring of the horsemen, but he had already called more than two hundred references and could only in good conscience hire three men who actually owned horses and would look good in thigh-high boots. None had handled swords, but they could learn, and they hated Jews and Christians. He was exhausted, but there didn't appear to be anything else the Antichrist had been working on. His phone rang.

"Randy Jarvis here," Buff said.

"Hey, Buff, this is Simon, your leader. Randy's alive."

"Alive! How did that happen?"

"We don't know. It would make sense if the period he had been dead was in any way divisible by three, but it's not. But either way, we're not much better off. He's got total amnesia. At least he thinks he's six and is looking for his mother. Oddly enough, he also thinks he's a Christian, and he says that he goes to church, loves Jesus, and wants to grow up and be in youth group like his big brothers. We're trying to rehabilitate him, but it's a long shot. You still might be in it for the duration. How are things on your end? Do you have armies moving into the valley of Supergeddon yet?"

"So far I have three horsemen."

"Three?"

"Three."

"Well, what about the armies?"

"I can't find the phone number for any armies. Randy's address book is completely empty."

"Look through his computer."

"It runs in DOS and I can't find a single useful program."

"Hit 'C:' and then 'dir.'"

"I tried that."

"What does it show you?"

"It lists 'castle.exe' and 'donkey.exe.' They're both games."

"So what did you do?"

"I played both of them. You know, computer games really have degenerated. These old DOS games are classic."

"I wrote a couple DOS games once."

FOUR

THE LAST CHAPTER STOPPED. THIS ONE IS
JUST STARTING.

*Further along in the Great Tribulation. Probably
about two weeks.*

RANDY HAD JUST finished sweeping out the tent and was
putting the broom away when Simon walked through
the flap.

"Randy," he said. Randy jumped and turned, his
face red. "Randy, we talked about this, didn't we?"

"Yes, sire."

"Don't call me that."

"Yes, sir."

"Were you sweeping?"

"Yes, Mother always told me to be helpful. I like
to take out the trash and sweep and things."

"You took out the trash too?"

"Yes, sir."

"Randy, this may not make sense to you, but it is
not at all helpful for you to try to help us. We have
other people who can do those things. But you can

help us. Do you want to help us?"

"Yes, sir."

"Do you know how you can help us?"

"By being evil."

"Right. We need you to be evil. If you're evil, then Christ can come back, and we can all go to Heaven."

"Could I go to Heaven too? If I helped and was evil?" Randy asked. His eyes had widened, and there was almost, nearly almost, the twinkle of the dawn of hope in the southern iris of his eye. But not quite.

"Um . . ." Simon said. "We'll talk about that later. Right now it's time for your lessons."

"Sir, I don't like my lessons."

"What would your mother say to that?"

"She wouldn't like them either. She would whip me for my lessons."

"Well, come on," and Simon took him by the back of the neck and led him out of the tent.

Randy sat at his special table inside the Sunday School tent. Across from him sat Hannah Shinymoon. She was an Indian R.N. who had fallen in love with the former resident computer genius who had been killed off to make room for Chang. I really couldn't say what was supposed to have happened to her in these books. She, like Haddie, may have died (it turns out that Haddie did die, so Simon had her sent home), or the author might simply have forgotten all about her

82

after killing off her love interest. But times were getting tough. The date that Simon had set for the hugest battle ever was fast approaching, Randy was making all the wrong kind of progress, and Buff was not impressing people with his work. Thus far he had only signed thirty-two horsemen, which he seemed to find impressive. Simon was stressing out, and his sermons were beginning to show it. Many suspected that he, with the arrival of the new laptop, had succumbed to temptation and was simply preaching through the "Knowing the Last Days" sermons from homiletics.com. He seemed to be buckling a little bit and was in no position to carp or criticize when it came to former cast members working out of book. He hadn't even asked Hannah about it, and she now had a regular shift working with Randy on his lessons.

Even now, right after that last paragraph ended, she pulled a canning jar out from her scrubs. It had the metal lid on it, but holes had been punched to allow the free passage of air. Inside it were grasshoppers. Two or three of them. Hannah had argued quite strongly with the council about the technique she was now hoping to use. It was her idea, that if Randy appeared to have lost all trace of evil and regressed in age, then he should be walked back along the path of corruption that most boys took. Beginning with torturing insects she hoped to get him quickly up to listening to rock and roll, and from there make the easy jump to pure, unadulterated God-hating. For now, she just had to get the jar of grasshoppers open, but the lid was sticking. Randy had to help her. When it was off, she spoke.

"Take the little one out." Randy did. "Pull its legs off, starting with the big jumpers."

"I don't want to."

"But you have to."

"Why?"

"Don't ask questions; just do what I say."

"But how will it jump?"

"It won't. Pull its legs off."

"I don't want to!" Randy yelled and began weeping. "Run, little grasshopper! Run!" he said, and tried to free it. "Jump!" he shrieked. But the grasshopper just sat in his open palm. Randy tried to move his hand but he was too slow. Hannah had reached across the table and slapped her hand on his. The little grasshopper was no more. There was a brief scuffle for the jar, but the other grasshoppers were bigger, and apparently more intelligent. In the end, they gained their freedom.

Once they had moved beyond the Hannah threat, Randy and Hannah picked themselves up off the floor breathing heavily.

"Randy, you are not helping us."

"I helped the grasshoppers."

"But God doesn't care if you helped the grasshoppers. He cares if you help us. He is not happy with you right now. But you don't care what God thinks, because you're evil."

"I don't want to be evil."

"You are."

"But I don't want to be evil. Sometimes I do bad things, but God forgives me."

"What kind of bad things?"

"Once I asked mother for a dog, and she said no, and then I was bad."

"What did you do?"

"I stomped my feet and said that I wanted one."

"Then what did you do?"

"I cried and said I was sorry and hugged her, and she said that Jesus forgave me and that I was washed clean." Hannah sat there for a long time just staring at him.

"Your mama was a liar," she finally said. Then she stood up. "My shift's over," and walked out. When she was gone, Naomi came in. She was holding a tupperware full of ants in one hand and a magnifying glass in the other.

"Hello, Randy!" she said. "How are we feeling today?"

Al was slowly climbing the temple mount on hands and knees. He was waiting to be incorporated into the story. He was sure he would have been yesterday, but oh well. So he was just passing the time. He had never crawled up the temple mount before.

Buford was walking from one place to another in Tetra when he bumped into Simon, for the first time out and about without the megaphone.

"Hello, Simon," he said.

"Hell, Buford."

"Hell-o. Don't forget the *o*, Simon."

"Right. Things aren't going too well, Bufe."

"I'd kind of gotten that impression."

"Randy won't even kill an insect. He won't do anything wrong other than sneak around behind our backs and clean the tents."

"He's cleaning tents?"

"Yes, and he empties trash cans wherever he can find them. But no, he won't even kill an ant. I mean what chance do we have of getting him fully operational and getting on track for Supergeddon? When I was his age I was forcing snakes into garden hoses head first and then cranking up the water."

"How old does he say he is now?"

"I don't know. We haven't asked him. You think we should?"

"Cleaning tents doesn't sound like a six-year-old. Maybe he didn't really get into trouble until his teens. Who knows, he could wake up eighteen tomorrow, and we could be back in action."

"Simon, can I talk to you?" Both men spun around. Randy had walked up behind them pretty dang sneakily.

"Sure, Randy. What about?"

"Girls. I'm kind of curious about this whole cycle of life thing. You know, babies and things."

Buford and Simon looked at each other, nodding slyly.

"Sure, Randy. I can meet you back at my tent in about twenty minutes."

"Thanks," Randy said, turned and walked off.

"Well, that's a good sign," Buford said. "What happens when the Antichrist notices girls? I think we'll be right on track."

"If your putz of a son-in-law gets anything done. My original estimation for Supergeddon is four days off, and his entire army consists of thirty-two horsemen and a marching band he's flying in from a Division II school in Louisiana. Division II! There's no way we'll be able to make this look convincing. Do you have any Valium?"

———————————

Buff's feet were on his desk. He hadn't really ventured out of his trailer since arriving. His fridge had been left fully stocked, and there was nothing to do outside other than watch the occasional moaner feel his way past in the brownness. Most of New Babylon's tenants had actually made it outside the city and its darkness by using an old Boy Scout technique called walking in a straight line. But there were still a few who didn't seem ready to leave.

He hadn't found too much to do, and he was getting bored. He was also getting sick of Simon. He called him every day to see if he had two hundred thousand horsemen yet, or if the armies of the world were moving into place yet. The truth was that Buff didn't think that he would ever be able to do something like that. He didn't know what he would do.

His phone rang again, perfectly on cue. He checked the caller ID and saw the old familiar number from Simon's tent in Tetra. He wouldn't answer. But Buff's eyes fell on the something else that he had not noticed: all the little memory buttons down the side of the phone. There were tons of them, and many of them bore catchy and interesting names. Three down from the top there was a button that said 'Armies.' Directly above that button, next to the one labeled 'two,' was written 'Emergency Conference.' He didn't want to try the 'Armies' button mostly because he didn't want to give Simon the satisfaction. So he reached over and hit the conference button. He sat in his chair waiting to hear a ring, or other traditional phone noise. But traditional phone noises were not to be had. Instead, in the distance, and growing louder, he heard a spectacular siren, shrieking like the lone platonic bat trying to find its way. He'd been dreaming a lot about that bat lately.

"Shoot, cuss!" he said. "I wonder how many people will come. Will there be enough Dixie cups?"

"Mail call," Flo said, and shoved a letter through the bars. "From the Christian Writers Guild. They said there was something for you to fill out, so this must be it."

"Al here," Al said. If there is a fountain in the Old City of Jerusalem, he was skipping rocks in it. If there isn't, then he was entering a shop to buy some cheese. Either way, he answered his cell phone and spoke the words so meticulously recorded above. "Hey, Simon, what do you need?" Pause for realism. "Mind and body control for mammals? Got just the thing." Additional pause. "Dunno yet. I've got the necessary equipment. I'll FedEx it tomorrow but it won't be worth anything without the operations manual, and I only know one guy who might have it, and he's a real bad-bottom. He be spendy too, but I'll let you know. See ya, Simon."

Al was in the story.

"Randy, how old are you?" Simon asked. He and Randy were once again lounging on the faux sheep-skin of the leadership tent. Bruce and Buford were lingering in the background, far enough away not to intimidate the gentle Randy, but close enough to form opinions without really being able to hear.

"I'm almost thirteen."

"That's great!" Simon said, and he handed Randy a piece of chocolate laced with a cactus juice so rare that it doesn't exist. This juice was intended to reduce Randy's inhibitions and shyness. "Why did you want to talk to me about girls?"

"Because I'm interested in one."

"What do you mean, interested?"

"I mean that I think she would be a great partner to me in my life-calling."

"What is your life-calling, Randy?"

"Right now there are two options I am thinking about. The first is a rodeo clown, because they really seem to enjoy helping people."

"What's the other one?"

"Praise music. I think I have a real gift in both composition and performance."

"Who would you be praising?"

"God, of course. Listen: day, hay, bay, dismay, Bombay, ho-hey. I rhyme things real easy. That wasn't even hard for me."

"When you say 'God,' you don't by any chance actually mean Satan?"

"No, of course not. Up, cup, sup, the first part of muppet, trumpet almost, thrup."

"*Thrup*'s not a word."

"Well, *up* is a hard thing to rhyme. When are you going to tell me about girls?"

"What specifically would you like to know?"

"How to get one."

"Well, you have to impress them. Or make them feel sorry for you. It's best if both happen. Be funny around them if you can. I usually just try to exude a spectacular charisma around them and that seems to do the trick."

"So I should be impressive, easily pitied, funny, and charismatic."

"If you could do all those things, I'm sure you'd have no trouble at all getting the girl of your dreams."

"Thanks, Simon. I've got to run now." And he did. Run, that is. In his excitement he missed the tent flap and the whole tent lurched after him. His middle-aged yet thirteen-year-old self quickly dropped to the ground and slithered out beneath the tent wall.

"Do you really think that was a good idea, Simon?" Bruce asked. "I mean, I have a fourteen-year-old daughter out there, and I hardly want the Antichrist, chalk full of seduction tips from the prophet of the millennium, sitting beside her at the campfire tonight."

"Buford, Bruce was never as quick as we were. Do you see what I was doing?"

"You want him to sin with a girl. You're hoping he will spiral down to the lowest pit of hell, using fornication with one of your own flock as the springboard that begins the descent."

"Well, I wouldn't quite put it that way. But I hardly see that one girl's virtue is more important than all of our souls. Besides, I expect to have this taken care of before he could actually do anything anyway."

"How's that?" Buford asked.

"I have something in the works. We'll talk about it in the next leadership meeting."

———————

Buff scurried around his trailer, straightening things up. His visitors, whoever they were, may not be able to see how clean he had made it, but they could at least appreciate not tripping on anything. Right when Buff was shutting the closet on the vacuum, he heard the first knock on the door. When he opened it he found a very small man standing before him. His pants were on backwards.

"Come on in," Buff said, and the man did. It was a little strange for Buff watching the man walk up his steps with the seat of his jeans bagging in front, but he was hardened and well trained, perfectly cool in all situations, and he handled this one nicely.

"Your pants are on backwards," he said. The little man snapped his head toward the noise, and there was hatred in his eyes.

"Who are you to say? You are just as blind as the rest of us." Buff wasn't sure if he should admit being able to see, but he didn't want this sort of insubordination: he had to present a strong Antichrist front.

"I may be a little hindered in my sight, but your pants are on backwards, and I have the authority to say it. I am Antichrist."

"Your own fly is probably down, Antichrist." Buff zipped it quickly.

"No, it isn't," he said. He was glad that he could leave the room when the door thumped again.

Eventually five men had come to the trailer, and one woman who claimed that she was there to keep minutes. Her name was DCLXVI. [Ed.: I want her to somehow be equivalent to 666. I think prophecy is clear that the number isn't actually of the Beast of Revelation. Dr. Sock tells me that it is far more likely to refer to the Beast's secretary. I tried to make it clear that she is the secretary through the line about her taking notes. Do you think that's clear enough? My wife recommended that I name her Viv Ivins, because that's a VI, VI, VI, and apparently VI means six in, uh . . . Romanesque? Romanic? Whatever. But I don't think it really has the necessary zip for a fast-paced make-me-a-millionaire book like this. And plus, what's with the *ns* on the end? What's that supposed to mean?] When everyone had finally sat down around the dining room table (things were a little tight), the little man who had arrived first stood up.

"Allow me to begin the proceedings. We were summoned for an emergency meeting, but let us not forget protocol. Antichrist, if you would mind hollering out a little bit so we could find you in the dark—"

"Hey nonny nonny!" Buff said. As soon as he had said this, the little man dropped to his knees in front of Buff and, with some effort, finally located his right hand. When he had reeled the hand in, he pressed the thumb against his own forehead and then inserted it into his mouth. When he pulled it back, he began wiping Buff's thumb dry between his own neck and chin and said, "You have called and your thumb has come." The same sort of thing happened with the other council members and his pinky, forefinger, big middle, and ring finger. Buff found it amusing. "Not that I would ever enjoy this sort of thing," he told himself.

"So," the little man said once the proceedings were obviously over. "Why are we here? What's the meeting about?"

"Darn it," thought Buff. He hadn't thought of that.

———————

Night in Tetra was really the only time anyone enjoyed themselves. It was a time full of contraband food, campfires, singing, and friendship. In addition to all of this, and unlike Tetra's daytime, you weren't in danger of losing track of time and being turned into a sheet of fruit leather by the sun. The general grouchiness and spirit of easily-annoyedness faded, and people passed around drinks and marshmallows and formed backrub chains. Nobody goes to Summer Camp for any of the daytime activities, and it was the same way with Tetra. If it weren't for the nights of jollity, Simon would have been alone long ago.

This night, the night of which we now speak, was good in all the normal ways, but it was special in one, well, *special* way. This night was the first night that Randy really joined the campfire crowd. Hannah had given Randy her guitar as a reward for giving three complete strangers wet willies. He had spent the late afternoon getting his fingers acclimated, and when evening fell, he set out boldly into the campfire scene. He stopped at the first three and watched the dynamic. None of them seemed to be quite for him. They were primarily for preexisting couples practicing lip wrestling. The newer couples and singles fires were limited to leaning and back rubbing. These were the fires he was looking for, and the fourth fire was his first attempt. He didn't attempt to join the conversation, he just sat on a rock and casually began strumming. People smiled at him, especially the redhead across the way, and went back to their conversation. The redhead offered him a marshmallow and he accepted. He only pretended to eat it because he didn't want his singing voice hindered.

Randy the Antichrist was patient. He waited until he saw his opportunity, and then, when it came, he struck as hard as he could. It was a mere five second lull in talk, and he managed to insert "Let It Be" by the Beatles, with "slight modification," as he put it, by Randy Jarvis. With the crowd soothed and now comfortable with the idea of listening and singing along, he followed up with a song by the Cranberries— a little more obscure for a mostly Israeli-Jewish crowd, but still effective. His voice was riveting, even to the campfires surrounding them, as he cracked it all over the place, in a perfect imitation of an Irish girl.

"You are so pretty the way you are," he told them. And they believed him. It was time for an original composition. He laughed with his audience and they chatted all around. He told them what little he remembered of his life. Lots about his mother. Pity was readily available to all. He ladled it onto the ground in front them. They only had to pick it up. He waited until they asked him for another song. Then he sang. It was the most moving musical event since Promise Keepers had folded the first time. It cannot be replicated in mere prose. He sang backup for himself. He drummed a bucket with his feet, and his hands and the guitar acted out scenes from the Song of Songs. Someone placed a harmonica in his mouth, and he played that too. And he sang. Some of the words he used included, but were not limited to: just, cup, milk, oh-oh, sorrow, slipping, hell, hot damnation, rejected, hurly-burly, pickle, and itchy. He sang of his overwhelming desire for general goodness, and young kittens, and how he was stuck being the Antichrist and wasn't being allowed to pursue his true love for the soft and fuzzy. It was perhaps a little more successful than he had anticipated, and when he hung his head down in tears and wept on the guitar, he wasn't faking. Someone was rubbing his shoulders, and he knew it was the redhead. He hoped she wouldn't touch the back of his head. Finally he noticed that the place was completely silent except for his own sobbing. He looked up and around. Hundreds crammed in close around the fire. A large fellow, and formerly considered most boyfriendable, asked the first question. He had experience in these things, and knew that the only way for him to retain any degree of status was to get in on the misery of this guy, or even better, the conversion.

"Hey," this guy said. "Why don't you just convert? They can't control you, man. You gotta do what's free for you to do when you're looking at it. Just cause Simon Ben-T says you have to be the Antichrist doesn't mean that you have to." It was eloquently put, he knew.

"But I am the Antichrist. I really am. And there is nothing I can do about it. I have been chosen, selected for the job. Just cause I don't want the job doesn't mean I get to skip it. It just means that I'm being a bad Antichrist." With those words, even the memory of the former heartthrob was wiped out. He was done and he knew it. He turned and was the first to leave the circle. There was no point in counting the number of girls crying.

"How old are you?" the redhead asked.

"Right now about nineteen, but Simon says I am a lot older."

And so it was that Randy Jarvis was made praise leader for all of Tetra.

———————

Al rapped thirty-three times on the steel door, in a special pattern that I can only imagine was neat. A slot opened, head-high.

"Yeah?" the slot said.

"I'm here to see Mowgli."

"Ha!" said the slot. "No one sees Mowgli. Who do you think you are?"

"I am Al. You should know what that stands for."

"My apologies. Please forgive my disrespect of a top-three dealer." The door opened and an abashed man with an Uzi waved him in. He was shown into a waiting room. There were large fake fig trees in buckets of bark chips, but Al didn't notice this. He was scoping the security situation. When he was done, he glanced through some magazines, and ended up counting to thirty-seven as slowly as possible. He didn't finish before he was called in by the receptionist, but he tried to mentally mark his place.

Mowgli was in a great big elephant-ear chair. There was a woman with him. She was preparing a spot on his thigh for a tattoo. Mowgli was covered with tattoos, and all but a couple were faces, faces of people. His thigh was apparently one of the only blank spots.

"Hiya, Al. You know why people say I get these, don't you?"

"Yeah. So that you receive some of the attention that your parents always gave to your siblings."

"So that I can remember who I've killed!"

"Oh, right. Mowgli, I need to buy the standard

operations manual for the mammalian mind and body control hardware and software that I took out of Langley."

"How much you willing to pay?"

"I've got ten Rand on me."

"Could you turn your head to the side, Mr. Al?" the tattoo artist said. "You have a nice profile and I'd like to use that."

"Sure," Al said, and turned his head. "So how about it, Mowgli? Ten Rands?"

"Go ahead, Tisha," Mowgli said, "I'm just checking to make sure that my gun is full of blanks. It is. Right, Al, take a little look down this!" And he pointed the gun at Al's feet.

"How am I supposed to look down it, when you keep waving it around like that? And I can't really look down the barrel when it's pointed at my feet."

Mowgli raised his gun. "You will never have my manual." And he shot him. But not really. Just in the story. Al's body hit the floor in a small pile. Somebody took care of him, I'm sure, as soon as the scene was over.

Al was back out of the story. Back in his trailer, he called his agent. He was not a happy monkey.

"FedEx for you, Simon," Chang said. He had just happened to be in the rocks near the entrance of Tetra when the truck pulled up. "I already signed for it."

Simon opened it immediately while Chang watched.

"It appears to be some sort of veterinary surgery kit," he said. "Oh wait. The box has pictures of a cat before and after. This should do nicely. Chang, will you run this to the leadership tent? I have to head over for my afternoon sermon."

"Sure," Chang said, and he did.

———

Buff's first meeting had gone very well, and he had called several others just because the whole finger ritual amused him. He had revealed to his cabinet everything he knew about Tetra, and had given orders for several strikes on the home of so many Jews. He had also begun calling the armies of the world. Most of their secretaries pretended like they didn't know who he was, and insisted that they would not under any circumstances "relay an order to whichever old guy is in charge and tell them to send every last man they have to the valley of Supergeddon." So far he had a very noncommittal total of five hundred peace keepers, and they would be coming from all over the globe. Of course the time frame allotted for Super-geddon was shot to heck anyway. What was another six months? Buff's phone rang. There was no need to check the ID. Simon was the only one who ever called him. The armies never called back.

"Hello, Simon," Buff said.

"Buff, was that you last night?"

"What do you mean?"

"Last night someone totally polluted our entire supply of manna. I though I was the only one who knew where it was kept."

"It's those huge plastic tubs labeled 'Nilla Wafers!' back behind the stage by the air guns."

"What air guns? I don't know about any air guns."

"The air guns you use to fire the stuff on the crowd."

"Buff! I pray, and it descends from Heaven. But you're not answering my question. Did you do that?"

"I didn't think they would actually do it. But we discussed something like that at one of my cabinet meetings. I thought we were just brainstorming."

"And 'Randy Jarvis Rules!' has been spraypainted all over anything that couldn't run away, and some that could."

"That definitely wasn't us."

"Well, do you think he would do that?"

"Maybe he has fans within the camp."

"No, that's not possible. Were there any other things that came up at this brainstorming event you held?"

"Not that I'm going to tell you. If they're going to do them, I should let them do them without interfering by giving you a heads up. You're the one who told me to be objective and neutral."

"Plotting our destruction is not neutrality."

"What would Randy do?" Buff asked, and he hung up. He'd never done anything like that, but it felt good to hang up on Simon. The phone rang again, and he picked it back up.

"Simon, stop bothering me. You'll see my teeming hordes soon enough."

"This is Russia," a voice said on the other end. The accent was not too convincing, but Buff worked with it.

"What can I do for you, Russia?"

"Specifically, this is a voice representing the armies of Russia. We have traditionally been associated with the role of supplying evil armies. I have been asked to inform you that this will be the last time we will submit to such usage. However, we are prepared to make this Supergeddon thing convincing. The entirety of our population will be in place in the valley by morning."

"Your whole population? But how will they fight? Do they all have guns?"

"No, but the sort of numbers you are requesting would be impossible otherwise. Most of them will be armed with pitchforks and scythes. Do not underestimate the Russian peasant."

"Tomorrow morning, you said? Well, that's terrific, I'll see you there. Tell your leaders thanks from me."

"You tell them yourself—they will be there. I said our entire population, and it will be our entire population. Good bye, Mr. Jarvis." Buff hung up the phone in disbelief. This thing might happen after all. The phone rang again. He was expecting Mexico or some equally daunting country, but it was Simon.

"Buff, someone torched the Wailing Wall last night in Jerusalem. Did you do that, Buff?"

"I just may have recommended it. Why?"

"You bastard! That was totally inappropriate! You are such a pathetic Antichrist, Buff! And I have news for you. The leadership met last night. Due to the fact that Supergeddon is now nearly a month late, I'm afraid we're going to have to let you go."

"Ha! And who are you going to replace me with?"

"Randy. We'll have him operational by this evening."

"No more cleaning tents?"

"Well, actually he cleaned tents all morning. Right now he's on stage, doing a few sets of secular covers, and then he'll move into his own praise songs. He's actually quite good. I can hear him from here, and he can really make that guitar groove. Most people are there listening. It's been helpful, as nobody seems to have noticed what you did to our manna yet."

"What's he covering right now?" Buff asked.

"Hold on," Simon was silent for a few seconds. "'Love Shack.' Earlier he did a great Dave Matthews."

"Wish I was there."

"You will be shortly. You can come back tonight."

"I can, but I won't."

"What?"

"You can't fire me, Simon. I'm going to see this through. I'm the Antichrist now. And do you know what, Simon? I'm going to make sure you burn."

"Buff, you can't do that. The leadership decided."

"Fine, send Randy out. He can't see in the dark. I'll kick his little has-been bottom."

"Buff, I will come for you personally and drag you back."

"Try it, Simon. Bring your fleshy self over here, and see what I'm capable of. I am called to rid this planet, and specifically Tetra, of all your type, and I will do it."

"Think of Cleo, Buff."

"I have. Why do you think that I have been swallowed by despair? She's gone from me, Simon. She's appearing in ads advertising conferences that will help more people write tripe like this. She's teaching workshops and reading other people's work. If she were dead, that would be one thing. I would know that I would see her again if I behaved. But she's not dead. She will be the president of the CWG when the millennium is ushered in. Then there won't be any death. She won't die. She'll be president for a thousand years! Do you think that sounds appealing? No, I'm ready for the Endgame."

"Endgame? What's that?"

"Shut up, Simon. Go tend your flock, listen to Randy play his music. Enjoy your last few hours of existence."

"Are you threatening me?"

"You've always been a quick one, Simon." Now Buff had hung up on him twice, and he was feeling great. He shouldn't need more than the entire population of Russia to get the job done. He leaned toward his phone and pushed a button, a button he had just reprogrammed. Something had been scribbled out next to it, and above had been written, in a handwriting Buff's sixth grade teacher would have recognized immediately, "Horsemen." When he pushed it, he heard the PA system of New Babylon kick on. The feedback gradually settled back down, and then, in the deepest voice Buff had been able to record, he heard himself say, "Saddle up!" It gave him terrific satisfaction to know that all through the park, one hundred and sixty-two horsemen were scurrying around in the dark looking for their boots.

Buff walked to the hall closet by the front door of his trailer. He pulled out two boots, both of black leather, a red cape, an enormously fat belt, and his helmet. He hadn't been able to fit any pants into his thigh high boots, so he was just going to wear his red boxers and tuck them into his boots. He dropped his pants and began pulling on his boots. The first slid nicely onto his left foot after only fifteen minutes. After another fifteen minutes, he was about into the second boot, but something was terribly wrong. It took him a minute, but he finally figured it out. Both boots were for left feet. Oh, well. No real surprise that the Antichrist would have something like *that* going on. He hopped up and hobbled around the place. He then removed his shirt and donned his black lined red cape, clasping it around his throat with a chain he had bought from a booth in the mall. The chain was very wizardy. Two little goblins gripped the cloth on both sides and the chain attached to their feet. In the center was a large, cloudy, plastic crystal. He had been tanning in preparation for this day, and he knew that when his cape blew back at a full gallop, he would cut an ideal figure. Lastly he put on his helmet. The helmet was from the Viking school of helmet fashion. There were two large horns and a nose guard, but more importantly, he had had two thick blond braids attached to the back. Then, dragging an eight-foot scabbardless sword behind him, he exited the mobile home. Beneath the carport lean-to on the side, a black stallion pony chomped at the bit, foamed at the mouth, and rolled its red eyes around in his skull. He had been very well trained. Buff mounted this black monster and, dragging the heavy sword behind him, trotted out into the road. His steed easily avoided the speed bumps. Three horsemen sat blindly waiting for him.

"The day has come!" he yelled, but his voice cracked horribly on 'come.' It felt like he'd lost a tonsil. "Where are the others?" He asked, and looked around him. Everywhere as far as he could see in the brown, lone horsemen were bumping into trailers and trampling shrubs. "Over here, you twerps!" he yelled, more carefully this time.

Chang and Naomi sat on a rock, clasping hands and

legs and things. Something in the air, and the way the blue sky just sort of gracefully burned into a sunset transition, told them that this was their last night on earth.

———————————

Simon stood in the center of the crowd and looked up at Randy. Randy had swung the guitar around behind his back and was delivering an altar call in a way Simon had not thought possible. But he knew things would change pretty quickly around here. He felt horribly betrayed by Buff, but wasn't sure why no one else seemed hungry. He turned and began the long trip through the crowd to his tent. He would go blog. Blogging always made him feel better.

———————————

"Randy, we heard your testimony tonight. It really is the most impressive testimony ever. The former Hell's Angels we usually use have nothing on you," Bruce said.

"Well," Randy said, "many men have been anti-Christ but very few have been the Antichrist. I feel like the Apostle Paul. He got knocked off a donkey by a blinding light; I slipped while running."

"You're more important than Paul," Simon said. "You obviously love God, but if you are actually converted then this is an event almost as big as the resurrection. Who knows what could come of your conversion? You are—or at least were—indwelt by Satan, you know."

"I didn't know that," Randy said. "When did that happen?"

"In the book after you were assassinated and then resurrected from the dead by Satan himself. It was at that point that you ceased being merely the Antichrist and became the Beast as well. Your own soul was replaced with Satan's."

"Satan has a soul?" Chang asked.

"Chang, what are you doing here?"

"You'll need me later."

"Oh right," Simon said, and he continued. "That's why your rededication last night—it was a rededication, wasn't it? Good. That's why your rededication has us wondering. Did your first soul come back? Do you have an entirely new soul that has converted? Or did Satan himself convert? Scripture only says that people who took your mark couldn't repent; it doesn't say explicitly that you can't. How does that make you feel, by the way? How does it make you feel that you are personally responsible for the damnation of billions?"

"Well, I was just an instrument of prophecy, and actually, as you have already pointed out, it radically improves my testimony."

"Right. Well, if you don't mind, we'd like to take a look at that head wound of yours. We think it might answer our questions about who you really are,

soul-wise I mean. Not that we doubt the genuineness
of your repentance."

"Well, if I repented, and you believe I did, then
aren't I automatically forgiven?"

"Not necessarily," Simon said. "You see, in some
books I've read about this sort of thing. There are
some people who just waited too long to repent. Then
one day, they are truly sorry, and repent of their sins
and trust in Jesus Christ, but God doesn't listen. He
hardens their hearts in such a way that no matter how
hard they try to repent, it doesn't work."

"But I feel great. Doesn't that mean that I'm in?"

"Well, we think so," Simon answered. "But we
want to make sure we get a real answer that we can
give to people in the congregation who have questions. So would you mind too terribly if we took a
look? You would receive local anesthetic and the
actual examination would be performed by Hannah
Shinymoon and Chang Wonton."

"Chang? Hannah's a nurse, but why Chang?"

"Well we had another nurse, but she totally flaked
on us in this book, and didn't even show up. Chang's
good with computers, so I can't imagine that the
requirements of neurosurgery would be beyond him.
So how about it?"

"Sure," Randy said, and he hopped up onto the
table. "Is this where you want me?" Chang nodded
and gently rolled Randy over onto his face. Hannah
then inserted a large needle into his spinal column.
When its juice had been pumped, Randy's body

quivered and went limp.

"Well," Simon said. "No going back now."

"Why not?" Bruce asked.

"I'm not sure. We couldn't get the actual instructions for this equipment, but there's something on the box about killing the cat unless something or other in the brain is snipped.

"The bridgy thing," Chang said. "You have to snip the bridgy thing."

"Simon, you said 'cat.' Why did you say 'cat'?" Bruce asked.

"Because this is actually designed for a cat, but Chang is pretty sure he can download an upgrade online."

"Shouldn't be a problem," Chang said. "Wow!"

"Satan has definitely been here," Hannah said. She had just lifted the back of Randy's head off, and the group now stood looking at a mind that looked like it had been smoking two packs per day for seventy years. "It's covered in tar."

"Well we can't wait too long. Insert the chip, the left and right transistors, and the receiver. Make sure you get the right channel on the receiver, or he could end up doing nothing but humming Yanni."

Buff was surprised when he and his horsemen crested

the last hill and looked down on the valley of Supergeddon.

"That's a lot of Russians," he said. The entire valley was full, shoulder to shoulder. In some places they were two layers deep. "I don't know that we'll fit. Wait here and be ready to charge," he told his horse-men. "I'm going to go look for the chief Russian."

As the sun rose, Hannah and Chang collapsed into each other's arms. Simon and the others were asleep on the floor. Randy still lay face down on the table. He would be a stomach sleeper from now on, as there was a little curly-cue cell phone antenna sticking out of his cowlick. Chang had used it to hopefully extend the remote control range that they would be able to have with Randy. After twelve straight hours of stitching and gluing and attempting to reprogram and override default assumptions and human impulses of goodness, both Hannah and Chang were excusably tired. And we should also probably excuse the fact that they didn't pay any attention to the fact that they were now sleeping in each other's arms on the floor of the leadership tent. And maybe they weren't quite asleep, but who cares? It was warm and soft and comforting.

"Did I make it clear, Randy? This is the last time we will serve as the armies of Gog and Magog from the North. We've hired an image consultant and he recommends de-Gogging as our first priority." The head Russian was dressed in traditional Russian garb. Traditional garb consists of [Note to the editor: I'm not sure what to call those outfits that are painted on those little Russian dolls. You know, the ones where you pop them open and there keep being smaller dolls inside? Well, whatever they wear, he was wearing too].

"Sure thing," Buff said. "I'm pretty sure that this will be the last time any of us do something like this. Are you ready?" The Russian nodded. "Okay," Buff said. "I'm going back up to the other horses. When you hear me start barking, then charge. Is that okay? Make sure some of your people go burn down the Old City of Jerusalem too."

"Fine."

Buff and his pony scampered off. Buff was still dragging the long sword behind him like a plow. Like a plow, get it?

"I would very much like a helmet like that," the Russian sighed. "But I do not have the hair."

When Randy woke up on the table, he threw his rear into the air and stretched every fiber of his being. He then hopped off the table and landed painfully on his hands and knees. First, he sat on Bruce's face. When Bruce stopped breathing, he moved on to Simon and licked his forehead raw. Then he tried to climb the pole at the center of the tent. Eventually things went wrong enough with that attempt that everyone woke up. It did take them quite a while to feel their way to the edge and squirm out. For some reason it took Hannah and Chang longer than the others. "There's something about really smart computer guys," Hannah thought to herself. "They're so snuggly."

Randy was outside sitting on a rock, waiting for them. It looked like he had been licking between all of his fingers, and there was something in the sand. Chang had to crawl back into the tent to find the remote control. When he got back out and handed the control to Simon, they both froze. Was that barking they heard? What could it be?

"Buff, you infidel!" Simon shrieked. "Quick, the whole valley is full of Russian peasants headed this way. Where's my bullhorn? Get the phasers mounted on the main deck! Buford, quick, find a four-wheeler and ride it around!" And still the Russians came.

———

Buff was bouncing awfully on his pony. But he could see Simon scurrying around on the rocks above Tetra. That's where he aimed his pony. He wanted to make Simon's nose bleed.

———

"Quick, hurry, hurry!" Simon yelled.

"Into the valley of death rode the six hundred!" yelled Buff.

"Ow! Oh, poop!" yelled Buford as he rolled his four wheeler off a cliff. He bounced around a bit and bled to death at the bottom.

"Cannon to the right of them!" yelled Buff, and his pony pounded on. He was barely outstripping the running peasants. His sword was uncomfortable on his right shoulder, dragging it like he was. He wanted to switch hands, but he also wanted to rumble with Simon as soon as possible. He was worried that switching hands would slow him down too much.

A. If you would like Buff to attempt to switch sword hands at a full gallop, please turn to page 115.

B. If you would like Buff to stand up in the stirrups and scream obscenities at Simon, turn to page 118.

ADVENTURE OPTION A:

Buff knew that switching sword hands at a full gallop was dangerous, but he had no idea that he could have cut his pony's head clean off. He flipped over the handlebars [Ed.: similar name for saddle thingy?] and received some nasty abrasions at the hands of the Middle Eastern rocks. He leapt to his feet, somehow still helmeted, and began running, or trying to run, up into Tetra. His two left boots gave him some real trouble, but his braids, it must be admitted, looked real nice flapping on his back. He left his sword behind and was now only carrying a small rock.

Simon was climbing higher and higher on the rocks. He had his digital camera with him, and he wanted to get the best angle of the clouds possible, to catch the glorious appearing when it went down. The Russians had reached Tetra now and were standing around looking at the Jews trying to rub the sleep out of their eyes and figure out what was going on. The horsemen had stopped as well, a little unsure what they should do with Tetra now that they were there. Simon kept climbing, and Buff was now hot on his heels, though he had accidentally dropped his rock. Simon reached a large rock, flat-like, and dropped to one knee, scanning the skies through his viewfinder.

"Where is he, Buff? Do you see him?"

Buff walked over to Simon and kicked him in the right shin.

"Ow! You ass! This is serious!" and he continued

his search of the skies. Buff reached down and twisted Simon's nose hard. It bled freely, and Simon no longer looked to the skies. He hopped to his feet and swiftly twisted Buff's nose, resulting in almost as much blood. Then they wrestled.

"I get it," Simon said. And then, "Whoof!" Four feet scurried. "We're both losing so much blood, only one of us will make it"—he paused as Buff's head butted him in the stomach—"to the glorious appearing. OW! Do you feel your heart palpitating? Is your brain losing oxygen?" Buff didn't answer. Simon had lost a sandal, and Buff grabbed two toes and pulled them as far apart as he could. Simon kicked him in the chin, and he bit his tongue.

They wrestled for quite some time. Eventually they could only lie on their backs and wheeze at each other.

"He's not coming," Buff said. "I'll send the Russians home." He leaned over the edge of the rock and waved at the head Russian. "Hey! You can go now! Thanks a bunch!" Then he flopped back over.

"I'm done," Simon said.

"Why?"

"Because I'm a false prophet. I was sure this would all happen. Now I have to go home. What will I do? My ministry is finished. I'll probably have to go to automotive school."

"Simon, nobody cares about false prophecy these days. I know ancient Israel took it serious, but nobody cares now."

"But my ministry. . ."

"Simon, people have been predicting this exact thing for centuries—respected people. Being wrong didn't hurt their ministries any. In fact it probably helped. Preaching the end gets people fired up. It doesn't really matter if anything actually ends."

"But I thought I was different from all of them. I thought I had it right."

"Well, try again."

"Thanks, Buff. I think I might."

"There's no might about it. Your theology demands it. Your kind of religion requires that you light your hair on fire and run around in panicked circles. Otherwise you're not seen as zealous."

"Well, what about you? It's your religion too."

"Not so much. I've decided to become Methodist. Either that or Anglican. I think I'll trade in my panic for a thick layer of dust. I've been too stressed lately."

"How will switching denominations help?"

"Oh, I have an uncle who's Methodist. Nobody ever expects you to act like you believe anything you say. I can't help but think that would be terribly restful."

"Best of luck to you, Buff," Simon said. "I mean it. I might try my hand at writing."

"Hey Simon!" a voice rose out of the valley beneath them. "Could you throw down Randy's control? I don't think we want him doing this in the sand right here."

THE END?

Adventure Option B:

Buff stood up in the stirrups and screamed obscenities at Simon.

"Infidel!" Simon responded. "It's the Pit for you, Buff!" And he picked up a rock to throw at Buff. He was high already, and he put everything he had into his throw, which of course meant that he overbalanced and fell off the cliff to his death from loss of blood. But the rock he threw went exactly where he wanted it to. It hit Buff in the Adam's apple and he fell off the back of his pony, unable to breathe. He coughed lots of blood. Too much blood. "Ah," he thought to himself. "I'm dying. My jugular has been ruptured beneath the skin and it is draining into my stomach and lungs. I remember Cleo when she was thin. I remember our young love, and our first cookie. It was I who encouraged bad dietary habits. I was always pushing for cookies! Forgive me, Cleo!" The last thing he remembered was the earth shaking. Then he died. He died very poetically, with lots of good description.

When he opened his eyes again, Simon was yelling.

"No! Oh no! I knew there was a slight possibility. I've read the book of Daniel, but no!" And he broke into sobs. Buff sat up.

"What's wrong, Simon? I thought we died. Where's Heaven?"

"We didn't go," Simon said. "We reverted to the previous save."

"You mean like in a computer game?"

"Yes."

"So we're not dead?"

"No."

"Well, that's good. When was the previous save?"

"1312."

"Oh."

"We'll probably be picked up by some slave traders soon and sold in the nearest market. So we will be dead soon. If you hadn't botched prophecy so badly this would not have happened. The world would have ended, and we would be in high-level government positions in the millennial kingdom."

"I never did like Buford. It's just like him to run at the pool."

THE END?

EPILOGUE

Half a league! Half a league! Half a league!
Into the valley of death rode some people.
Cannon to the right of them! Other dangers to their
    left!
Hey nonny, nonny and a hot cha-cha.

See the next book for our
surprising conclusion. . .

IN ONE HUGELY DISTURBING MOMENT
THE WORLD'S CHRISTIANS AND ALL ONE HUNDRED PERCENT COTTON HAS BEEN SUCKED TO AN UNDIS-CLOSED LOCATION. THE WORLD IS LEFT WONDERING WHY THE AVERAGE ADULT I.Q. HAS SKYROCKETED.

Experience the adventure for yourself, but make sure your bladder has been emptied beforehand. The not-so-bestselling Right Behind™ series is now available in soft cover, no cover, several difficult foreign languages, and a special clothing-optional version.

1. RIGHT BEHIND
A Parody of Last Days Goofiness. Also available in French as *Les Behindes*.

2. TRIBULATION FARCE
Evangelicals off Broadway

3. AGRICOLAE
On Early Roman Farming

4. LOCUSTS AND YOU
A Guide to Preserving Your Garden in Troubled Times

5. FENG SHUIING THE END
How to Arrange Your Cosmic Battle

6. ASSONANCE
Assignment: Devotional Poetry; Target: Vowel Repetition

7. STALLING FOR TIME UNTIL THE NEXT BOOK
Ho-hum, tra-la-la, bum-te-dum-te-dum

8. BIRTHMARK
The Beast Gets Shy

9. THE DESECRATOR
Rumbling in the Ring with the Biggest Pig Ever

10. THE TENEMENT
One Below Supergeddon

11. SUPERGEDDON
A Really Big Geddon

A Serrated Edge:
A Brief Defense of Biblical Satire and Trinitarian Skylarking
by Douglas Wilson

Satire is a kind of preaching. Satire pervades Scripture. Satire treats the foibles of sinners with a less than perfect tenderness.

But if a Christian employs satire today, he is almost immediately called to account for his "unbiblical" behavior. Yet Scripture shows that the central point of some religious controversies is to give offense. When Christ was confronted with ecclesiastical obstinacy and other forms of arrogance, he showed us a godly pattern for giving offense. In every controversy, godliness and wisdom (or the lack of them) are to be determined by careful appeal to the Scriptures and not to the fact of someone having taken offense. Perhaps they ought to have taken offense, and perhaps someone ought to have endeavored to give it.

For more books in *The Upturned Table Parody Series* visit http://www.canonpress.org, or call 800-488-2034.

Right Behind:
A Parody of Last Days Goofiness.
by Nathan D. Wilson

The Mantra of Jabez:
A Christian Parody
by Douglas M. Jones

The Upturned Table Parody Series

The "upturned table" in our series name points back to Christ's anger with the merchants in the temple. Our parody series isn't as concerned with money in the Temple as it is with what modern Evangelicals spend on abject silliness. Now you can't say that sort of thing or publish parodies without someone pointing out that you're no genius yourself. And we don't claim to be. First, we see our parodies as sermons—to ourselves before anyone else. For we too are responsible for the lame state of popular Evangelicalism today, even those of us who are from more classical Protestant backgrounds. We, too, exhibit some of the targets of our own barbs. Second, we also don't claim to sit aloof, all clean and wise, looking down on others' silliness. We are a part of the Evangelical community ourselves. These are our brothers who write these things; they represent us too. We have no doubts about their sincerity and good-hearted goals and wonderful characters, but we all must do light-years better.

The first response from many who love the books we aim to skewer is to be "wounded" and "offended," but that is the tiresome refuge of every little god who thinks blasphemy restrictions apply to him (oooh, notice the evil gender violation there). We all need to grow up and take the heat. But what about all those for whom these "precious" books have meant so much? One answer is that medieval folks could say the same thing about their relics. Relics made people feel warm and fuzzy too, but they were evidence of sickness.

Christian reality is a rich and fascinating blend of truth, beauty, and goodness. It is an exuberant love of life and light and celebration. Even with some of the glorious heights of Christian culture reached in prior eras, the Church still hasn't truly begun to plumb the magnificence of the Triune God. We're only scratching the surface, all the while non-Christian visions are perennially addicted to death. In order to mature, Evangelicals need to move beyond the bumper sticker shallowness of the past four decades and long for true wisdom. Parodying our silliness is one small nudge in that direction. *To whom much is given, much is expected.*